NORWICH
in the 1970s

Ten Years in the Life of the City

PETE GOODRUM

For Andrew and Stephen, the eternal bond

First published 2015

Amberley Publishing
The Hill, Stroud
Gloucestershire, GL5 4EP

www.amberley-books.com

British Library Cataloguing in Publication Data.
A catalogue record for this book is available from the British Library.

ISBN 978 1 4456 4563 6 (paperback)
ISBN 978 1 4456 4571 1 (ebook)

Typeset in 10pt on 12pt Sabon.
Typesetting and Origination by Amberley Publishing.
Printed in the UK.

CONTENTS

ABOUT THE AUTHOR

Pete Goodrum is a Norwich man. He has had a successful career in advertising agencies, working on national and international campaigns, and now works as a freelance advertising writer and consultant.

Pete is also a successful author. His books, *Norwich in the 1950s*, *Norwich in the 1960s* and *Norfolk Broads: The Biography*, published by Amberley, all topped the local bestseller charts.

He makes frequent appearances on BBC local radio covering topics ranging from advertising to music and social trends, and is a TV presenter. A regular reader at live poetry sessions, and actively involved in the media, Pete has a real passion for the history of Norwich and Norfolk.

He lives in the centre of the city with his wife, Sue.

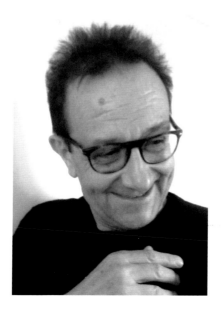

ACKNOWLEDGEMENTS

My thanks are due, as always, to several people.

Firstly to Andrew Wenley who, at the very outset of this project, kindly and enthusiastically shared with me his archives and memories, allowing me to reproduce pictures. Thanks, Andrew. Jonathan Plunkett has given me access to his father's photographs. George Plunkett's pictures of Norwich are a valuable insight into the city's history.

Thanks to Wayne Persinger and Lorraine Howes at Captain America's Hamburger Heaven. Your memories and permission to reproduce items from your archive are hugely appreciated.

I'm indebted to the team at Jarrolds, especially Jane French, for arranging to let me pore over their precious scrapbooks and to include pictures from them.

A special mention to my radio friend, Steve Bumfrey, who introduced me to Steve Lambert. And a huge thank you to Mr Lambert for sparing the time to give me an insight into Norwich in the 1970s – and the punks!

It was a great pleasure to meet Jonty Young, and my thanks are due to him for finding, and reproducing, images from the 1970s. Thanks too to Dave Gutteridge for the introduction.

Paul Harley kindly helped with pictures.

Thanks to Anna Stone, Group Archivist at Aviva plc for her help and permission to reproduce items from their files.

A special mention to Wayne Beauchamp who gave me access to pictures from the North Walsham and District Community Archive, which includes photographs of Norwich by Les Edwards.

To everyone who helped – thanks.

I have made every effort to track down and obtain permission for the use of all the material in this book, and duly given credit. If there is anything in these pages that you believe belongs to you and I've not given credit, it's only because I couldn't find you, despite every effort to make contact. Some of the organisations featured have obviously long since disappeared. Please accept that I've used the material in good faith to help tell this story, and that I've done so with gratitude and respect.

My gratitude to the team at Amberley Publishing for their continued help and support.

And, as ever, a very special thank you to my wife, Sue. It can't be easy living with a writer, and I owe her enormous gratitude for her constant support and understanding. Thanks, Susie!

INTRODUCTION

For some, the 1970s meant punk rock and political unrest. For others, it was a time of Abba and affluence. The decade's dual identity was as striking in Norwich as it was nationally. While once familiar streets were demolished, new buildings sprang up. Different brand names appeared in the city centre and with them came a new era of shopping and eating out.

This book is a look over the shoulder to the steakhouses and nightclubs, the fashions and trends that defined the decade.

Drawing on vintage advertising and many never before published images, this book is a fascinating glimpse, and reminder, of how we lived in Norwich in the 1970s.

Opposite: A view of Norwich. (Courtesy of Elliott Brown, under Creative Commons 2.0)

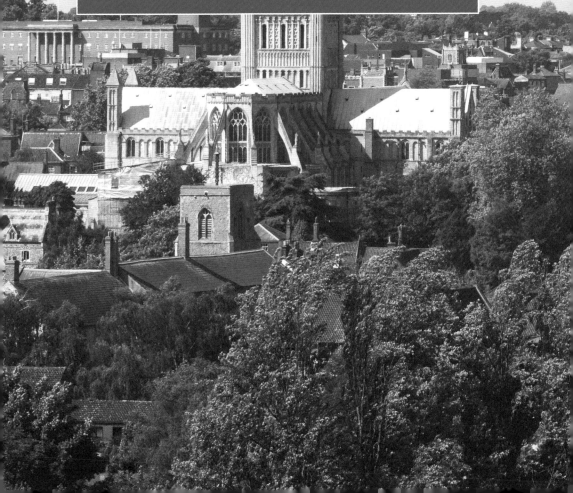

1

THE DECADE
BEGINS

1 January 1970, the first day of a new decade, was a Thursday. Still traditionally 'half day closing' for most shops in the city, this Thursday was not however a day off. It would be 1974 before New Year's Day became an official Bank Holiday, and many of a certain age will remember struggling to work on 1 January while suffering from the excesses of the previous night!

Thursday 1 January 1970 was a dull and misty day in Norwich. The forecast was for more of the same, with the threat of some snow showers.

If you had braved the weather, and made it into the city for some shopping, some of the delights that awaited you were a seasonally necessary, oil heater at Jarvis's in St Benedicts, for £7 19s 6d, and a plastic handbag at Bonds for 27s 6d. Full decimalisation was over a year away.

Crossroads dominated tea time television, and later on that Thursday evening the schedules offered *The Dave King Show* and *Survival*.

Not far from the television listings pages of the *Eastern Evening News*, you'd find the latest, usually mini-skirted, young lady featured as 'Our Girl Thursday' and she would in turn, on that particular Thursday, be not far away from the first of the advertisements for the January Sales.

In short, the very early 1970s in Norwich looked very much like the late 1960s in Norwich. No master switch had been thrown at midnight, propelling the city out of the previous swinging decade and into the ten years that would bring yet more changes. Norwich, like everywhere else, eased into the 1970s on a cold January morning, unaware that a decade later life would have changed forever.

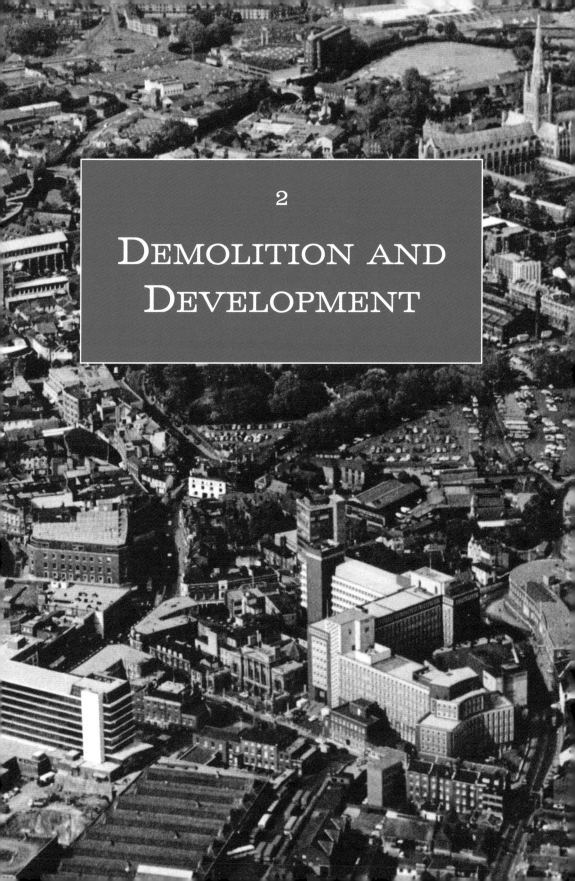

2

DEMOLITION AND DEVELOPMENT

The 1960s in Norwich had seen the city preoccupied with traffic, its effects and how to countermand them. While altering and improving the road system would continue during the early 1970s, it did so alongside the demolition of old and construction of new buildings.

However, the two strands overlapped, as did the two decades, in one of the city's most controversial developments: The Magdalen Street Flyover. Magdalen Street had been at the centre of an area of alleys, courts and tiny streets for decades. The housing was, in many cases, woefully outdated by 1960s standards and by then increased traffic was choking the main thoroughfare.

The area had been under scrutiny for some time, as the proposal for an 'inner link road' had been on the table since as early as 1944, and it had become more of a reality when plans were actually drawn up in 1965. In the meantime, during the 1950s, Magdalen Street had undergone something of a 'facelift', but it was to prove a temporary stage in the area's development.

Prior to the 1965 plan, there had been much discussion. One idea had been to widen Magdalen Street itself and build a roundabout, linking it to the inner link road. By December 1961 however, the City Council approved a plan to build what was then called a viaduct across Magdalen Street.

By early 1962, the *Eastern Daily Press* had already dubbed the project 'the Bridge of Sighs' and published a piece in which they quoted the Civic Trust as saying that 'the new development, far from destroying the character of the (Magdalen) street, gives it fresh interest.'

By that March they were reporting on a council meeting at which town planners had agreed that 'the flyover, instead of a ground level crossing, will save the destruction of a good deal of property.'

Opinions and emotions were already running high. Quoting the eminent architect Basil Spence, Mr Geoffrey Gorham wrote to the editor of the *Eastern Daily Press* to say,

Sir, the road vehicle is one of the greatest potential menaces to our civilisation from an aesthetic point of view and if Magdalen Street was freed from the brutalising effect of the motor car it would be a place people would want to go to (but) decapitated by an unwanted flyover it is a place where only planners would want to go.

Later the same month an architect's model and photographs of the proposed flyover were displayed to the public at City Hall, and by April the City Council had approved the plan. It was not an instantly popular decision. In the run up to the 1970s, the Magdalen Street flyover, and its implications, was never off the local agenda. There was public anger in 1963 when it was announced that, aside from a grant of £521,840, a further and seemingly necessary £173,950 would be borrowed, with capital charges of £13,000. The route of the inner link road itself remained under debate. The streets in question read like a litany of the areas of the city that would change in the coming decade. The government appeared to be ready to provide a grant, for a road between St Giles Gate and Barrack Street. Norwich City Council were anxious not to appear ungrateful, but were desperate to finalise the decision on the route. It said that the issue must be settled quickly as land had to be acquired and planning allowed to proceed on the basis of:

- The route proposed was the shortest and therefore likely to be the most attractive to traffic.
- It passes through an area where much traffic is generated and will thus best serve its purpose of distributing such traffic.
- The route provides convenient links to the radial roads.
- It does not pass through any primary residential areas.
- It is substantially less costly than the alternative proposals.

They expanded their argument by saying:

The Committee believes that the construction of an inner link road along this
route, as opposed to Oak Street, Bakers Road, Magpie Road and Bull Close Road
will enhance rather than detract from the value of Magdalen Street as a shopping
area.

There followed a pointed reminder that an earlier plan had 'envisaged
a widening of Magdalen Street which would have entirely destroyed its
character.'

Yet another route was brought into discussion by the Norwich
Society. They suggested that the road should run through City Station,
over a new river bridge, and on to Bakers Road, Magpie Road and Bull
Close Road, where it would join Barrack Street at Silver Road. They
were broadly supported by the Chamber of Commerce.

The Norwich Society found other allies in the Magdalen Street and
District Traders' Association, who felt that the scheme would have a
dramatic effect on their businesses, and not just affect the atmosphere
of the street but endanger St Saviour's Church. Consistent lobbying
of Parliament by both groups brought results. It led to the Ministry
of Housing and Local Government setting up a public inquiry. This
did not please the City Council who wanted to get on with the work.
Petitions were raised, questions were asked about the route or 'line'
of the proposed project. By 1965, the government was saying that it
favoured the plan for 'a five-span viaduct with East & West approach
ramps, high level access to Anglia Square made from reinforced concrete
with brick facing'. 1966 saw the Ministry of Housing saying point blank
that the decision to build could not be reversed. Work began in earnest
in 1967 and by 1969, with the 1970s fast approaching, May Gurney
was awarded contracts for substantial parts of the new road scheme,
including roundabouts at Chapel Field Road, Barrack Street, and Pitt
Street as well as the road from Pitt Street to Westwick Street. It's as we
enter the 1970s that the controversy, in many ways, reaches its climax.
Through the last days of the 1960s, money had been committed and

work had begun. With it came some serious revelations. The sheer size of the flyover started to become a reality. Five giant spans, precast concrete and high tensile bars didn't even sound attractive. Plans to build shops under the flyover seemed to be withering on the vine. It now emerged that, in an attempt to contain the amount of land to be purchased, the plans did not allow for any pedestrian usage of the flyover. The costs were rising.

By May 1970, public opinion was increasing in volume again. Quite simply people were asking if the flyover was actually needed. A council meeting, in all its heated argument, became a pivotal moment. As the voices raised in the council chamber, two things emerged. The council felt that whatever people felt, the project had gone too far to turn back. But, records show that everybody the Council included, now saw that the whole thing was a dreadful error: 'a ghastly planning mistake'. Among talk of reallocating the funds to another solution, the reality that had to be faced was that Sovereign Securities had already been given planning permission to commence work, close roads and buy up properties. There were fears that a U-turn would send the wrong signal to local commerce, resulting in confusion and chaos. The awfulness of the dilemma under debate in that council meeting is perhaps best summed up by the comments of Mr Harry Perry. To put his words into context, we have to understand that the city had changed during the long drawn-out years of the flyover discussion. Some of the thinking went all the way back to the 1945 report on traffic and post-war development. By the arrival of the 1970s, there had been another shift in the balance of city-based industry and residential areas. Circumstances had changed and Mr Perry alluded to that, and the nightmare they were all now facing, when he said that he was adamant 'that the flyover could and should be stopped now we have changed circumstances. For council members to say it is a ghastly mistake and still say it must go on is too silly for words.' He'd hit the nail on the head, and he created a furore. Was it, people asked, now a case of not inconveniencing Sovereign Securities and not upsetting their plans, even if we didn't want or need the flyover? It didn't stop anything. The construction workers called it 'May Gurney's Flying Circus'. The tons of steel and concrete poured in. Nobody had realised that the design meant the flyover was too short to allow the older, still in service, buses to go under it. Even Monty Gaynor, who led the design team, could see that it was unpopular. He commented wryly, 'Norwich will have its ultra-modern four-lane flyover. Whether Norwich takes to it is a matter for the future.' And the future was fast approaching. Anglia Square was opened. In the midst of talk of noise pollution and comments from the local press they closed Magdalen Street to put down ninety 30-ton beams, laying one every twenty minutes. It was accepted as a 'ghastly mistake', but it had proved unstoppable.

The Lord Mayor, Dick Seabrook, officially opened the flyover on 12 June 1972. The 1970s were barely started, and the city was not happy with how things were going.

While the building work for the flyover and Anglia Square dominated the Magdalen Street area, it was not the only place undergoing change and disruption. Some contemporary film footage shows the early 1970s city as a place of demolition and upheaval. It was progress at a price, and graffiti such as 'Restore don't demolish' and 'Hands off history' began to appear on walls. Older housing was knocked down. New council houses were built. Entirely new areas were built. As early as 1973, the city council had bought over 500 acres of land. The cost was £9.5 million and the plan was to build some 10,000 homes at Chapel Break, Three Score and Clover Hill. The first residents of Clover Hill moved in during 1977. The 1970s would see the building of a teaching centre, diagnostic facility and a new block for the main wards at the Norfolk and Norwich Hospital, which still dominated its city centre site.

Across the city, close to the site where the hospital would one day move, the still relatively new University of East Anglia was about to receive an extraordinary gift that would, in turn, create the need for another new building. In 1973, Sir Robert and Lady Sainsbury donated their collection of art to the university. It was a diverse and eclectic body of work and their adventurous spirit was echoed in their radical choice of the still young Norman Foster as the architect to design a home for it.   The Sainsbury Centre opened in 1978, and it was a revelation. Stunning in its external appearance, it delivered a new and breathtaking approach inside. Lord and Lady Sainsbury had not wanted a 'museum'. It certainly wasn't. Now, in Norwich, there was a place to look at art in a different way. It was at eye level. It was easy to see. It was groundbreaking.

In the same corner of the city, 1973 had seen the start of a project that would become the 'UEA Broad'. It would take until 1978 to excavate eighteen acres of gravel to create the Broad. In an innovative arrangement the company carried out the excavation for free, provided they left the Broad, fed by the Yare, for the university.

Meanwhile, back in the city centre, traffic was still an issue. It had dominated 1960s thinking in Norwich, and even now as the residential demographic changed, and building and demolition dominated the skyline, it was still high on the agenda.

Norwich had led the way with pedestrianised streets, and in 1976 it was in the forefront again. This time it was speed bumps. Perhaps a minor moment in history, but Norwich was only the third city in the UK to install bumps in an attempt to keep people to the 30 mph limit. Motum Road was perceived as an accident black spot and the 'sleeping policemen', as they were sometimes called, were placed at spaces of 50 and 150 yards along its length. They were seen as experimental, so much so that it was promised that they would be removed a year after their installation.

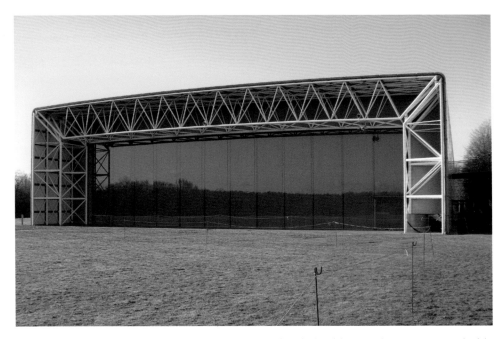

The Sainsbury Centre on completion. A remarkable building to house a remarkable collection. It's has also been featured in movies. (Photograph by Oxyman)

Drivers in the city would have been all too aware of the demolition that marked the 1970s. Sometimes it revealed fascinating glimpses into the history of Norwich. On Chapel Field Road, for example, motorists and pedestrians alike would have seen from the demolition sites that the Victorians had had no qualms about building terraced houses leaning against the ancient city walls.

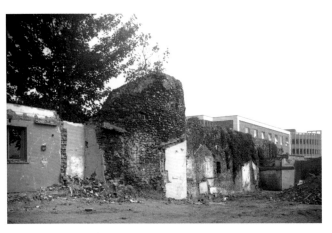

You can almost smell the chocolate! Caley's building stands in the background, as does the still relatively new multi-storey car park. In the foreground Victorian terraced houses are being demolished on Chapel Field Road. It's plain to see that they had been built directly against the city walls. (Photograph by George Plunkett)

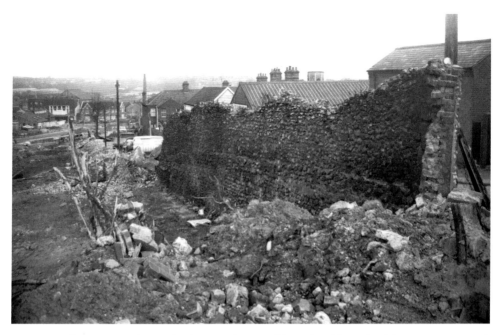

Grapes Hill in 1970 shows further evidence of how buildings had been constructed close to, and even using, the ancient city walls. (Photograph by George Plunkett)

This was an era of change. While new developments promised a brighter future the city was witnessing the disappearance of familiar landmarks.

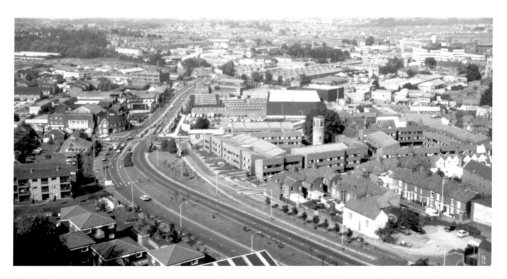

If evidence was needed of the changing city, this 1978 view, with the much changed Grapes Hill at its centre, is it! (Photograph by George Plunkett)

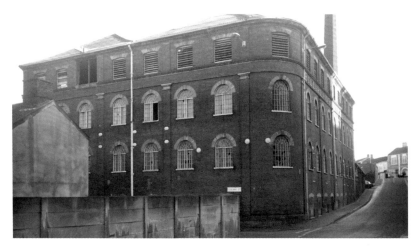

Approaching the end of an era. Bullards Brewery in 1973, showing signs of decay. (Photograph by George Plunkett)

Although the famous chimney would not be demolished until some years later, the legendary Bullard's Anchor Brewery in Coslany Street was not the force it was.

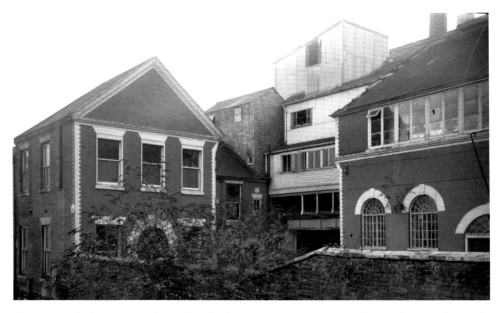

Just around the corner, the Bullards Counting House was still standing in the early 1970s. (Photograph by George Plunkett)

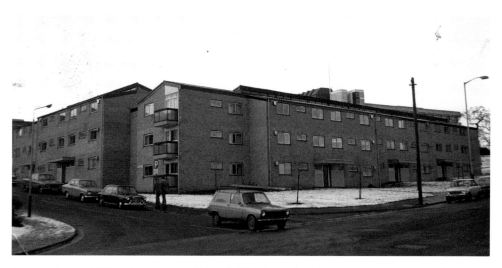

Rouen Road, 1970s. (Courtest of North Walsham & District Community Archive)

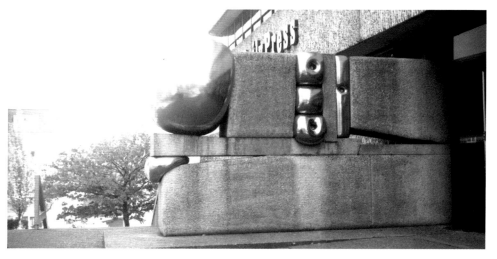

Professor Bernard Meadows' sculpture at the *Eastern Daily Press* offices, Prospect House, 1970. (Photograph by George Plunkett)

When Prospect House opened its doors in 1970 it heralded another chapter in the history of press production and the media in Norwich. However, it was not without controversy. The new building at the top of Rouen Road featured as part of its frontage a sculpture by Professor Bernard Meadows. It had been commissioned in 1968 for the projected new building and was reportedly inspired by the sign for the nearby Woolpack pub in Golden Ball Street. Entitled 'Public Sculpture', it attracted much comment, with the words 'belly button' often being used. It certainly made its mark on the Norwich architectural scene!

As the *Eastern Daily Press* embraced the 1970s it developed its role as a significant advertising medium, and many of the advertisements it ran – some featured in this book – were produced by the city's advertising agencies. In the 1970s, pre-eminent among those was Tibbenhams. Grown out of the old Willsmore and Tibbenham agency, Tibbenhams attracted talent from London and beyond to become a mainstay of the Norwich creative scene.

Much of the Norwich brewing industry operated from the Norwich Brewery offices in Rouen Road during the 1970s. Consolidation, mergers and takeovers had seen the demise of many smaller brewers and the 70s saw virtually total domination by Watney Mann. In the ensuing decades, a return to craft beers and small breweries would see a stark reversal of those 'corporate' times when some beers were produced which to this day provoke controversial, if not fond, memories!

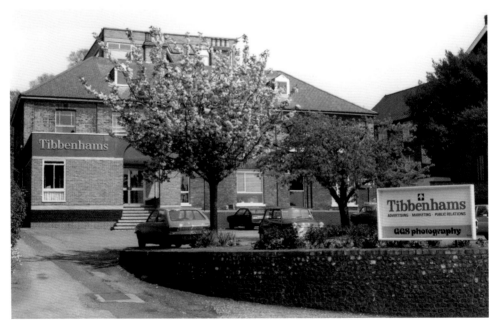

The Tibbenham building, Thorpe Road. The home of Tibbenham Advertising in the 1970s.

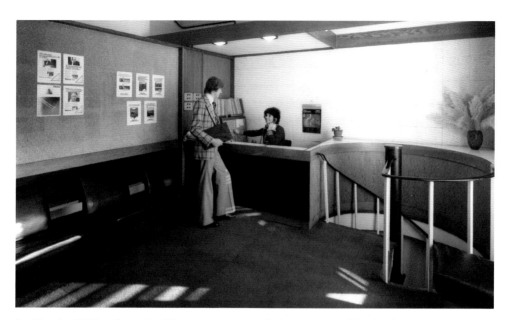

Inside the Tibbenham building *c.* 1974 and the new world of advertising agencies meant refurbishment – and flared trousers!

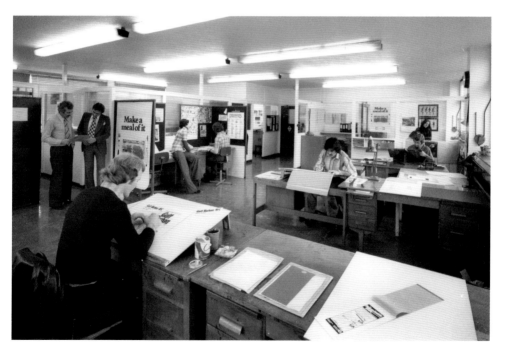

Tibbenhams, like all advertising and newspaper offices in the 1970s, was still in a pre-computer world. Commercial art was produced in studios, like this one, using techniques that had not altered much in decades. Magic markers and 'Letraset' were the order of the day!

Some attempt to establish a more local flavour was made in 1976 with the launch of The Norwich Brewery Company Ltd, but by modern standards this was still big-time beer production.

Rouen Road, at the heart of all this was an area of considerable change during the late 1960s and into the 1970s. New housing replaced many of the old terraced streets, the brewery buildings were extended, and at the top of the road the *Easter Daily Press* opened their new offices in Prospect House.

A vital part of the Norwich commercial scene in the 1970s was Norwich Union, as Aviva was still known at the time. Founded in the city and with centuries of growth and development to its credit, Norwich Union dominated much of the skyline. Many Norwich school leavers began their working lives there, many staying with the company throughout their careers.

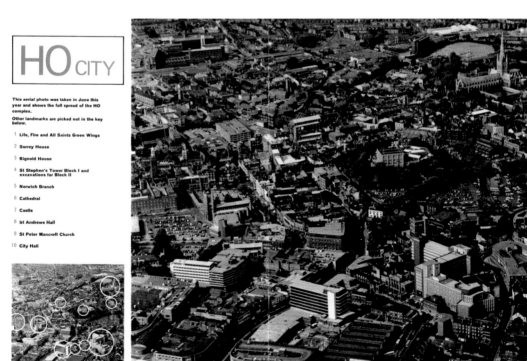

HO CITY

This aerial photo was taken in June this year and shows the full spread of the HO complex.
Other landmarks are picked out in the key below.

1 Life, Fire and All Saints Green Wings
2 Surrey House
3 Bignold House
4 St Stephen's Tower Block I and excavations for Block II
5 Norwich Branch
6 Cathedral
7 Castle
8 St Andrews Hall
9 St Peter Mancroft Church
10 City Hall

The Norwich Union staff magazine of 1974 showed this aerial view of the city, pinpointing the company's buildings. (Courtesy of Aviva)

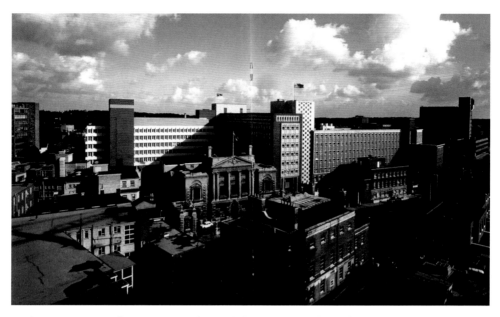

In the same issue, the magazine showed this picture which features the offices on All Saints Green. The changing skyline is as evident as ever.

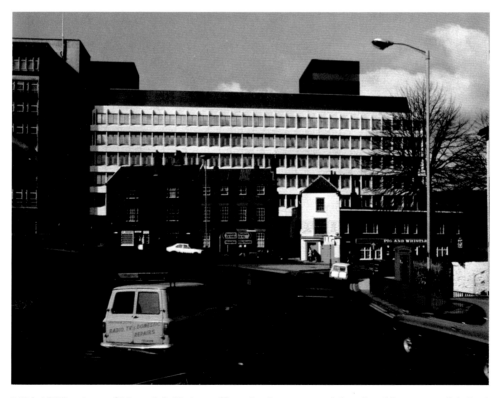

Mid-1970s view of Norwich Union offices in the centre of the city. (Courtesy of Aviva)

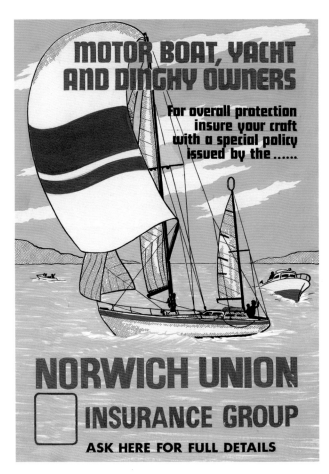

Mid-1970s advertising
for Norwich Union,
demonstrating the wide
range of insurance on offer.
(Courtesy of Aviva)

Another famous Norwich business site was to be a part of the
development of the city. Jewson had been established in Norwich since
1868 and it was where one of their timber yards had stood that a piece
of Norwich took a very 1970s turn.

Aware of a shifting pattern of where and how people wanted to live,
Norwich City Council in the 1970s was actively looking for ways to
encourage them to inhabit the historic central quarters of the city.

A partnership was created with local developers R. G. Carter Ltd and
in May 1972 planning permission was granted for a project described as
'the development of a builders' merchants premises by the construction
of roads, footpaths and twenty-four parking spaces and the erection of
forty houses (twenty-two with integral garages) at Colegate'.

What had been Jewson's yard would become Friars Quay.

Sitting among ancient churches and bridges, the development featured a range of terraces and open spaces that led down the River Wensum.

It's interesting to note that the planning permission contained some specific aims and conditions. They included protecting and improving 'the amenity of the area', and ensuring 'the maximum public use of the riverside'.

This was a critically acclaimed design and Friars Quay appeared, favourably, in *Architectural Review*.

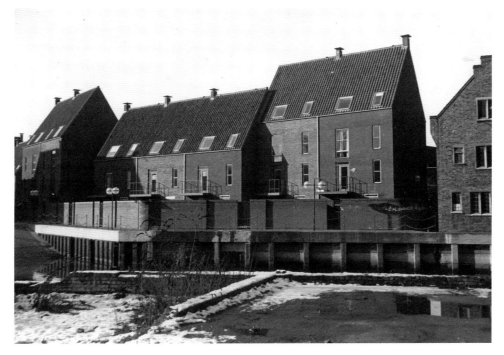

Friars Quay. (Courtesy of North Walsham & District Community Archive)

Friars Quay is seen here in stark winter light and, soon after completion, was a seriously modern development in an historic part of the city. It was soon a sought after address and in many ways typified the 'new look' of the city's architectural development. With forty four- and five-bedroom houses and some ground floor flats, the scheme included integral garages and extra parking spaces. All of it was just a stone's throw from Colegate where, in 1868, George Jewson had established the head office for his hugely successful timber business. George's son Richard, who would become Lord Mayor in 1917, went on to grow the firm into what has been reported as the 'largest timber merchants between the Thames and the Humber'.

With developments, roads, houses and commercial buildings all actively involved in this great transition, it's perhaps best to take a step away from the detail and look at the big picture. Norwich in the 1970s was taking on a different look and the following photographs give a panoramic view of the city and its changing skyline.

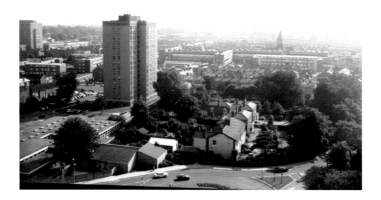

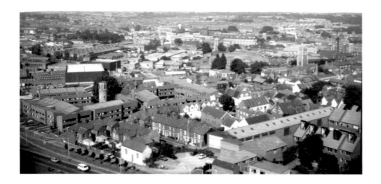

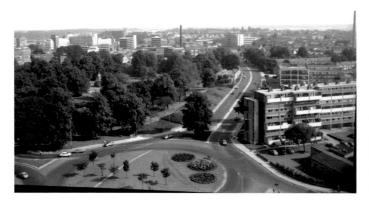

The city in 1978. Now there are tower blocks on the skyline. (Photograph by George Plunkett)

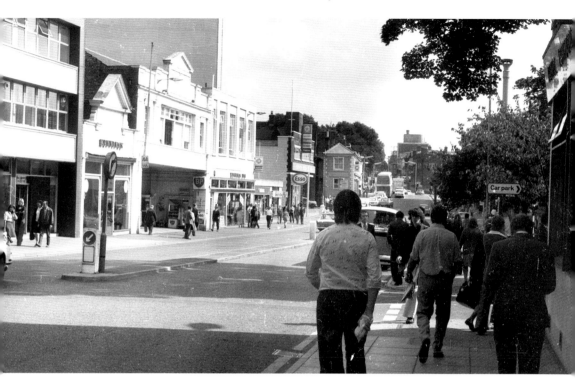

Prince of Wales Road, 1970s. (Photograph courtesy of Andrew Wenley)

Focusing in on one particular road it is possible to see just how the city was and had been changing. This mid-70s shot of Prince of Wales Road clearly shows how offices, petrol stations and traffic controls had altered the appearance of this busy road since its Edwardian calm. Some of the buildings in the picture sit uneasily with the planning and conservation that prevail today, but this was post-war, fast-changing Norwich and some of our more modern sensitivities were perhaps overlooked. The decorative frontage of the original Kennings building for instance sits hard against the more austere architecture of its next-door neighbour, while the slab sides of new office blocks dwarf the older buildings.

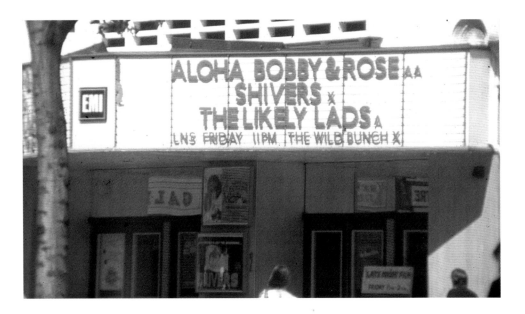

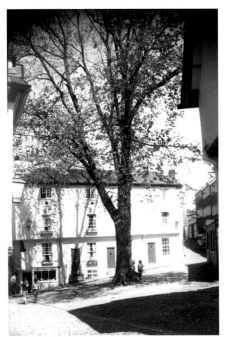

Above: A 1975 shot of Prince of Wales Road shows the ABC cinema and the hit films of the moment.

Left: Elm Hill, 1978. (Photograph by George Plunkett)

Opposite: Jarrolds at Christmas. (Courtesy of Michael Button, under Creative Commons 2.0)

In a final, wistful, note for this chapter on the demolition and development of 1970s Norwich, it's worth reflecting on the fact that it didn't just affect buildings. In this 1978 shot of Elm Hill the giant tree is still standing.

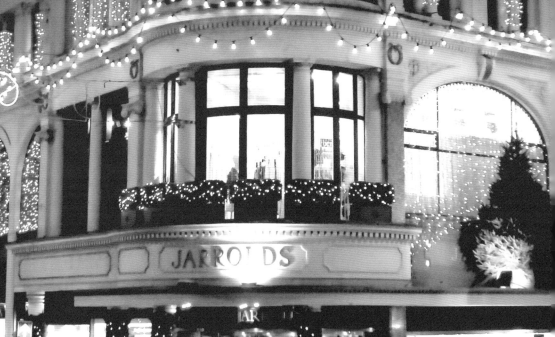

3

IN THE HOME

If the streets were changing, and old houses were giving way to new, creating a new exterior look to the city, what was life like inside the homes of Norwich in the 1970s? The 1960s had accelerated the social changes brought in during the immediately post-war 1950s. Homes had gained a modernity that fitted with the swinging decade.

Now, though, the very teenagers who had defined the sixties were growing up. They were getting married and buying houses. Saving up for your own house was still a relatively new aspiration. In many families, the 1970s saw a social mobility that had been unknown to previous generations.

Once, the bank and the building society had been institutions for the middle classes and above. Now young people across the social strata saw home owning as attainable and they saved their money to raise the deposits for mortgages.

Financial advertising came into its own as more 'products' were made available for the prudent and ambitious citizens of the 70s.

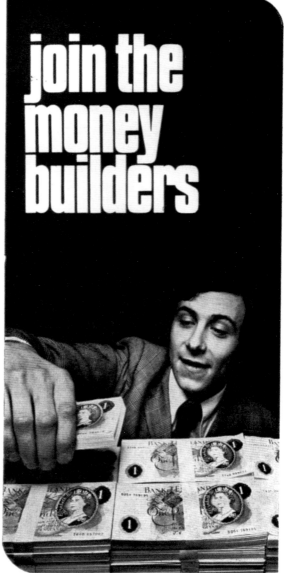

join the money builders

We are the experts when it comes to saving money. We make it grow safely and surely. Small or large amounts. Regularly or occasionally. Quick and easy withdrawal. Call in, write or phone to discuss the best way to invest your money. Open Saturday mornings.

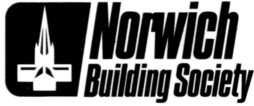

Norwich Building Society

Head Office:
St. Andrew's House, Norwich, NOR 54A Telephone Norwich 21367
City Office:
37a St. Andrew's St., Norwich, NOR 54A Telephone Norwich 23500
City Branch Manager: Mr. M. H. Crawford
Member of the Building Societies Association.
Shares and Deposits in this Society are Trustee Investments.

In Norwich, the Norwich Building Society was still just that. Pre-merger it was the city's own company. And it was even open on Saturday mornings!

Once they had a home of their own people now wanted a more sophisticated and more modern way of living. They'd been abroad and seen European style. The package holiday had a history dating back to the previous century, but by the 1970s it was the passport to international travel for a new generation. It would have an effect on how we ate and drank. It would widen the horizons of a post war generation who could now buy guaranteed sunshine. And it wasn't always about Spanish beaches. Ideas for new destinations were constantly promoted, as Norwich's own George Wortley pointed out.

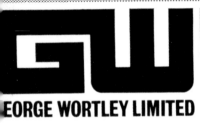

EORGE WORTLEY LIMITED

GEORGE WORTLEY LIMITED
International Travel Agents
CHARING CROSS, NORWICH,
NORFOLK, NOR 22J, ENGLAND
Telephone: Norwich 26254

85 Prince of Wales Road,
Norwich, Norfolk, NOR 01S
Telephone: Norwich 28481

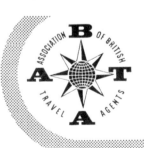

DIE SCHWEIZ   LA SUISSE
SVIZZERA   SWITZERLAND

Four ways of saying the holiday of a lifetime.

George Wortley are offering luxury eight-day holidays in Lucerne, flying direct from Norwich by DC9 jet. The cost is £56.75 which includes travel by luxury coach between Zurich and the Hotel Seeburg; accommodation in twin-bedded rooms with hot and cold water (single rooms available for a small extra charge); and a special Folk Evening at the Lucerne Casino.

And the one way to go is with George Wortley.

Above: Holiday advertising in the 1970s – check out the prices – and by DC9!

Opposite: Seckers for refrigerators, and Woodhouse for furnishings. And Orford Hill still has a red telephone box! (Photograph by George Plunkett)

National magazine and, increasingly, television advertising promoted more ideas for holidays than ever before. When the holiday-makers returned home they brought more than the traditional bull fight poster and straw donkey souvenirs, though. They brought ideas for the way they lived. They brought ideas for their homes. And they expected to find what they wanted in local retailers. Norwich had never been short of retailers, and shops such as Jarrold's, Garland's and Bond's had amply provided for the city's homemakers for decades.

Specialist furniture shops had always been part of the Norwich retail scene, and included names such as Brett's, Tasker's and Wallace King.

And of course, in St Benedict's, there was Henry Jarvis. Many Norwich folk have the fondest memories of that store, with its labyrinth of departments. In St Stephens there was the Co-Operative, an organisation with a proud history and an eye to the future. Still retaining its customer base who had grown used to saving for their dividend or 'divvy', the Co-Op was modernising, aiming to capture the new generation of home makers.

The picture says a lot about the decade. Shop frontages were being revamped but the overall architecture wasn't perhaps getting the attention it deserved.

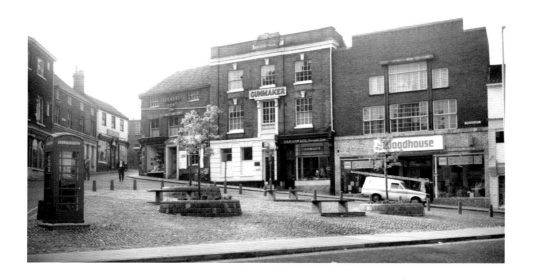

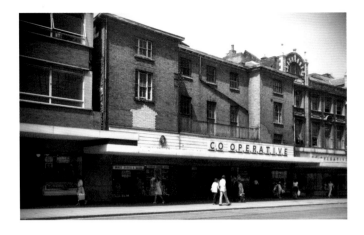

The 'Co-Op', St Stephens, 1970s. (Photograph by George Plunkett)

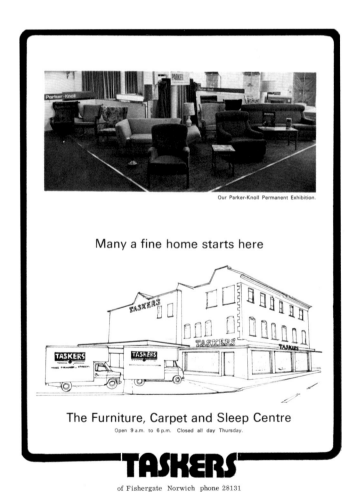
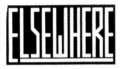
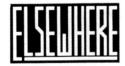

Right: Jarrold's, 1970s.

Opposite below left: Tasker's of Fishergate, 1970s. A little short on content perhaps, but this advertisement says a lot about the tone of the 1970s with its simple, but aspirational line – 'Many a fine home starts here'.

Opposite below right: Even more in keeping with the spirit of the moment was advertising from smaller retailers, like this from Elsewhere in Dove Street. The name of the shop defines the new approach. Not a founder's name but a trendy brand, and a message that spoke directly to the new, more adventurous and more discerning homemaker.

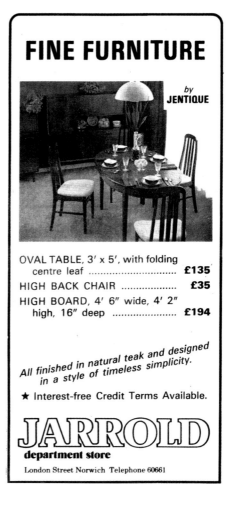

FINE FURNITURE

by **JENTIQUE**

OVAL TABLE, 3' x 5', with folding
  centre leaf **£135**
HIGH BACK CHAIR **£35**
HIGH BOARD, 4' 6" wide, 4' 2"
  high, 16" deep **£194**

All finished in natural teak and designed in a style of timeless simplicity.

★ Interest-free Credit Terms Available.

JARROLD
department store
London Street Norwich Telephone 60661

Accessories such as cutlery and glassware were all very well of course, but despite changing fashions there was still the need for the essential furnishings. Jentique, a major brand in the 1970s, was available through that essential part of Norwich retailing, Jarrold's. The prices in this mid-1970s advertisement are interesting. So is the still relatively traditional approach to having a dining table and chairs. TV Dinners would change the way we lived, but this central feature of the home was still something aspired to by the majority. What's most telling is the reference to 'natural teak'. It was the look that said so much about the 1970s home. It said you were more modern than your mum and dad!

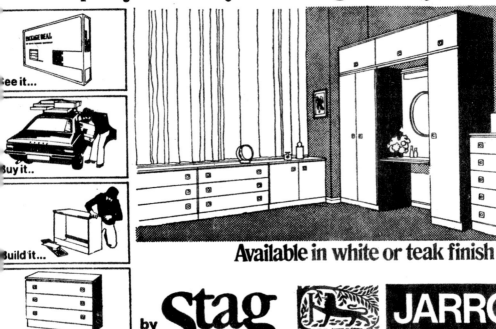
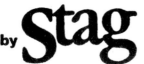
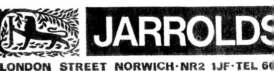
They may have been upholding some traditional values but Jarrolds were certainly in
the forefront of new ideas too. We may not have yet discovered the joys of a certain
giant Swedish retailer and all that flat pack would bring, but the 1970s saw the arrival
of self-assembly furniture. Available in very modern white, or the fashionable teak,
STAG furniture was something you could, as the advertisement proudly proclaims,
'bring home in your car today'.

The method of construction was new, but so was the style. This was the bedroom
for the generation who no longer wanted their parents' dressing table and wardrobe;
this was the look they'd seen in the magazines and on TV. It was the style they'd found
in their overseas holiday hotels. In fact the headline approach to this advertisement is
more than a nod to the package holiday.

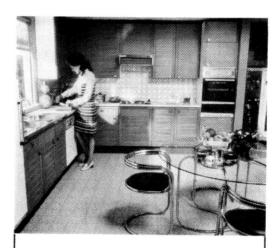

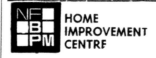
High on the list of aspirational brands for the homemakers of 1970s Norwich, as it was across the nation, was HYGENA.

If STAG was offering a new look to the bedroom, HYGENA was the name for kitchens. Branded to be as modern as possible, HYGENA 2000 pitched itself at the twenty-first century. In the mid-1970s the year 2000 seemed a long way ahead!

But this was the complete luxury kitchen. Deliberately mounting a counter attack on the new-fangled self-assembly furniture, HYGENA kitchens offered everything the 1970s family wanted. It's doubtful that a phrase like 'the most beautiful kitchen in the world' would pass the legal standards of today's advertising, but the overstatement is forgivable now. The product itself, and Gunton and Havers' offer of seeing it in a room setting, would have been hugely attractive.

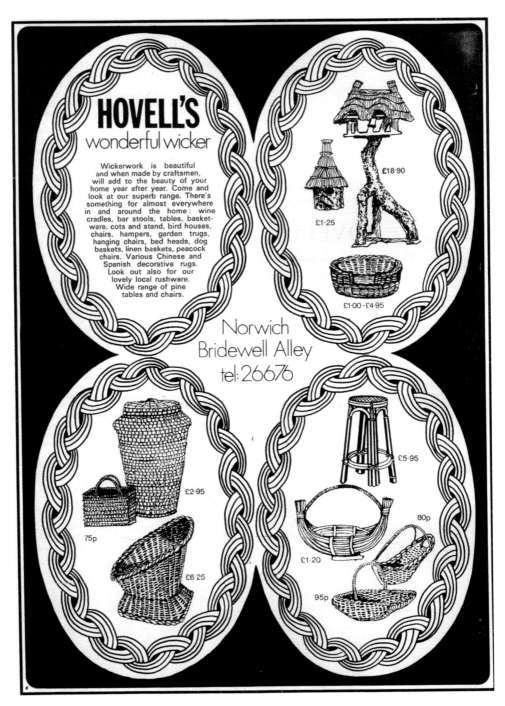

Very much part of the 1970s interiors look was wicker. And nobody did wicker better than Hovell's in Bridewell Alley. The 1972 prices are interesting!

It's impossible to look back at furnishing the home without mentioning Queensway. This Norwich company was instrumental in pioneering the national trend for what would become known as 'out of town shopping'.

Gerry Parish was demobbed from his National Service in 1950 and after a few jobs, including asphalter and tiler, he found work as a carpet fitter at what was then still, in the pre-John Lewis days, Bond's. By the mid-1950s he'd gone into business with his brother to form Parish Brothers, selling furniture and carpets.

He opened Queensway as a shop in 1967 on Queens Road.

It was a visit to his sister in the USA that gave him the idea. He saw that the future of carpet and furniture retailing lay in a warehouse style, offering big discounts to the consumer through outlets that were not the traditional city centre shops.

He moved quickly, taking on a disused warehouse as premises and immediately implementing his strategy of offering hefty discounts, and investing hugely in advertising. It worked. The advertising fuelled ever increasing sales, which gave him the buying power to negotiate bigger discounts from manufacturers and suppliers, which he passed on to customers. By 1971, Queensway's sales were running at more than £18 million a year, and they were opening a new branch every month.

By 1977, Queensway was on track to be floated as a public company with a value in the region of £7 million. It wasn't to be. A drop in profits, exacerbated by the economic downturn of the times, meant the flotation was withdrawn. Struggling with his health, Gerry Parish sold Queensway to Harris Carpets.

Queensway was not his only venture and Gerry established other businesses, including the Oasis Sports and Leisure Club. Just as he had with furniture and carpet retailing, he'd been a forerunner with a service in a market that would soon be the norm.

He was inextricably linked to the city's cultural life too, having invested in the Jacquard Club, which opened in 1971. There he frequently performed, playing harmonica, with co-founder, the legendary Albert

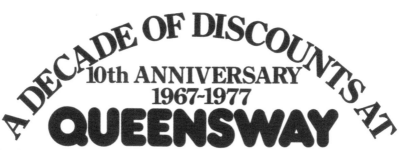
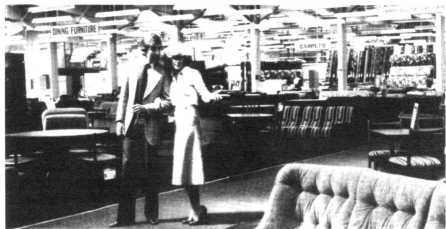
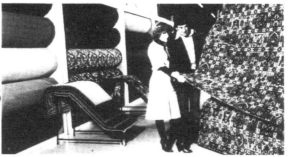
Queensway, 1977.

Cooper. But his legacy really lies with Queensway. One of the great brand names to have come out of Norwich, and somewhere that many people setting up home in the 1970s would have been to for 'choice, quality, low prices and good furnishing value'.

With the living room, bedroom and kitchen suitably and fashionably furnished, what were we doing for home entertainment in the 1970s? Television had long since established its dominance as the main medium. The giant mains radio (or wireless) had given up its pride of place to the transistor, and the demographics of radio listening had changed. The 'pirate' stations that had defined alternative teenage tuning in during the 1960s were gone.

TV ownership had increased dramatically as had colour TV. It would be a long time before we were logging on to shop and play games online, but for the technically savvy, up to date family of the 1970s there was – Videomaster Visionscore!

From their shop in Castle Street (and others in the region), Visionhire were actively protecting their traditional market of renting televisions. This had been the accepted practice for years. The traditional argument had been rooted in there being no costs if the set went wrong. It wasn't yours, so you called the repair man from the rental company and he came and fixed it as part of your agreement. Increasing affluence and falling prices were eroding that, but Visionhire had a secret weapon! Rent a new 22 or 26 inch colour TV and you got the Videoscore game – for free!

With a choice of three bat sizes and random midfield players, 'in the case of soccer', this was high-tech entertainment at its best.

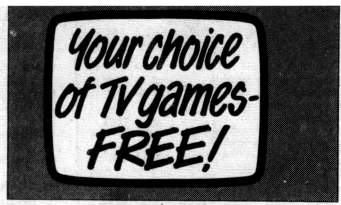
Before computer games, there was the Videomaster Visionscore – from Visionhire!

Happily playing your TV game with the two remote controls, in your stylish 1970s home, you may of course have still hankered for some of the old traditional aspects of home life. In the 1970s the Solid Fuel Advisory Service was very keen to extol the virtues of the 'real fire'.

While some, even then, saw this as a fashionable piece of retro living, the main motivation for the campaign was to help the nation's then difficult energy problems. This advertisement, which appeared in Norwich in the 1970s, tells several stories.

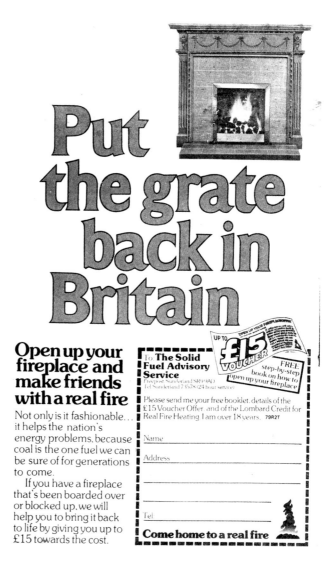

Put the grate back in Britain

Open up your fireplace and make friends with a real fire

Not only is it fashionable... it helps the nation's energy problems, because coal is the one fuel we can be sure of for generations to come.

If you have a fireplace that's been boarded over or blocked up, we will help you to bring it back to life by giving you up to £15 towards the cost.

UP TO £15 VOUCHER

FREE step-by-step book on how to open up your fireplace

To: **The Solid Fuel Advisory Service**
Freepost Sunderland SR99AD
Tel Sunderland 7 5678 (24 hour service)

Please send me your free booklet, details of the £15 Voucher Offer, and of the Lombard Credit for Real Fire Heating. I am over 18 years. **79R2T**

Name

Address

Tel

Come home to a real fire

The 1970s – and the Solid Fuel Advisory Service tell us how to be both fashionable and aware of the growing energy crisis.

'Put the grate back in Britain', for all its clever punning, was very much influenced by the earlier 'I'm backing Britain' campaign. The ad's message strikes home. Raising interest in a younger audience, it refers to a real fire as being fashionable, but wastes no time in getting to the national energy problem. It goes on to mention that you might have a fireplace that's 'boarded over or blocked up'. How many households had done that in the late 1960s at the beginning of the new modernity that would accelerate through the 1970s?

All in all, it's a commendably well-presented argument, tuning in precisely to the trends, social factors and marketing pressures of the time. The one sentence that stands out as being so much of its time, and so understandably unaware of what the future held is, 'because coal is the one fuel we can be sure of for generations to come'. Who knew? Perhaps, if TV games weren't your thing, you might like to sit, possibly in front of your newly reopened coal fireplace, and listen to music. The 1960s had seen dramatic improvements in record playing equipment, but the 1970s saw 'Hi-Fi' come into its own.

Most Norwich department stores catered for the trend, and many were the homes that became proud owners of a teak effect record deck, complete with its smoky glass lid. From Wilmott's in Prince of Wales Road to Bond's and beyond, you could buy the various makes and models of Hi-Fi, sometimes upgrading them with different speakers, and accessorising them with all manner of gadgets to remove the dust from your precious LPs.

But, if you were serious about it there was only one name that counted: Martins.

After a brief period as 'Mick Helps', the small shop on Ber Street emerged as Martins Electronic Centre. Initially selling government surplus, Mike and Ted Martin soon discovered the demand for Hi-Fi. Legend has it that a student called in to the shop and became the catalyst for the brothers to assemble a complete Hi-Fi system for sale, as opposed to the kits of parts they'd been selling.

These were the days of bands recording ever more complex albums to be listened to in ever more sophisticated stereo, and Martins delivered the kit. The business grew throughout the 1970s, opening new branches and increasing their stock of speakers, turntables and amps to meet the demands of a growing and devoted customer base.

Many an LP was played in many a 1970s Norwich home on equipment bought from Martins.

To close this chapter on the home, and the retailers who helped furnish it, we must return to the start of the decade, and a tragedy. Garland's was an integral part of Norwich life. The department store had long been a favourite with London Street shoppers. On 1 August 1970 a fire started in the kitchens. It spread rapidly.

It had been less than thirty years since Norwich suffered the war time blitz, and to many the scene following the Garland's fire must have had an eerie similarity to some of those 1940s mornings after air raids. Damaged beyond repair, what was left of the building was taken down.

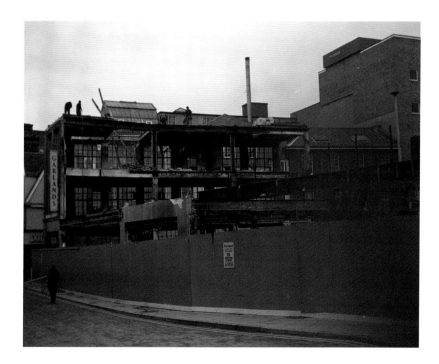

Garland's, after the fire. (Photograph by the late Les Edwards and courtesy of Wayne Beauchamp)

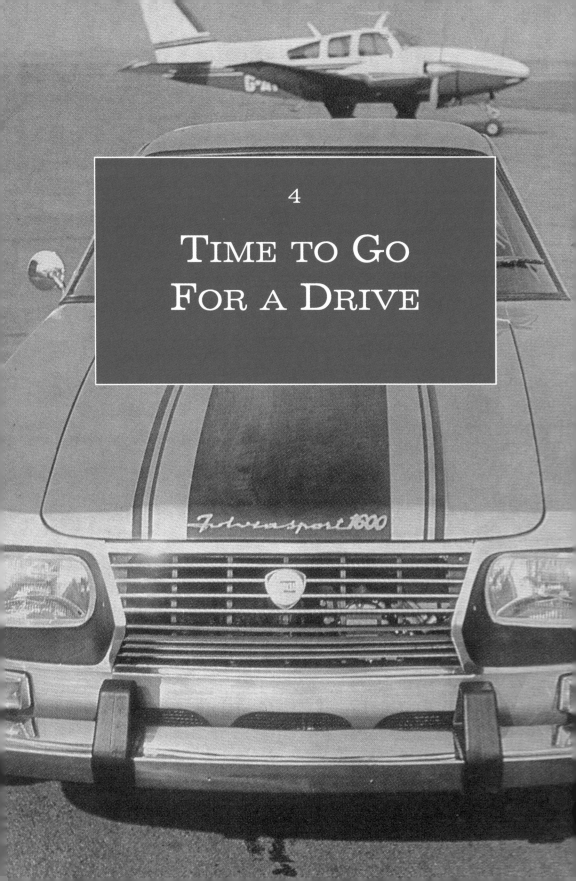

4

TIME TO GO
FOR A DRIVE

If the home was becoming more sophisticated, the other great aspiration in the 1970s was the car. It might have been the root of the traffic problems that had preoccupied the city from the end of the war and through the 1960s; there may have been energy concerns for the country, and even pollution issues were beginning to be recognised, but this was the 1970s. Upward social mobility was the order of the day, green issues were not high on the agenda and, to be frank, status symbols were important. Everybody wanted a car – and possibly two.

Evidence of the two-car family aspiration is brilliantly captured in this 1970s ad from AJS on Whiffler Road. Running with the national campaign from Citroën's Dyane it's not, in terms of political correctness, an approach that would pass muster today.

But, seen at the time, it captures so much of the prevalent trends. Referring directly to cars being bought to impress the neighbours, it quickly takes in independent suspension before covering the low fuel consumption and low price.

Our bowler-hatted (this was the 1970s!) owner, is then reminded that – wait a minute – maybe such a clever buy *would* impress the neighbours, so he'd better not let his wife take the credit.

By any standards it's amusing, if not scurrilous, by modern standards, but it does sum up the attitude that, in the 1970s, said that a successful family had two cars. (But that the wife was secondary!)

None of this reflects on the motor traders of Norwich. These were the attitudes of the times and Norwich was, as it is today, a thriving place. The arguments over certain road developments and architectural mistakes took nothing away from the city's ability to keep pace with the nation.

It's true that that the Citroën advertising unashamedly featured the surprisingly low price of the Dyane, but it was done almost as a novelty approach. Unlike today, when cars are often advertised on how to pay for them, with attractive finance deals being the main selling point, the 1970s was an era where older, established motor car marketing methods

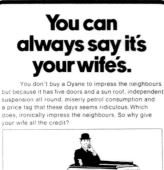
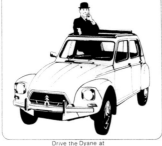

It's the 1970s and AJS Limited carry Citroën's message to the aspirational families of Norwich. It wouldn't work today!

ruled. If you were at home, sitting in your Jentique chair, watching your rented Visionhire television, your onscreen heroes – especially if you were a bloke – were the high octane, macho characters of *The Sweeney* and similar shows. Cars mattered.

The Pointer Motor Company's ads of the time capture the era beautifully.

Yet again continental influences are important. So is performance. Luxurious appointments come next – because you're a discriminating motorist. Of course the price is mentioned – and compare them to today if you will! – but there's no attempt to say it's a bargain. You've arrived. You can afford it. This is the 1970s; you deserve it!

The new Zagato bodied Lancia Fulvia Sport 1600

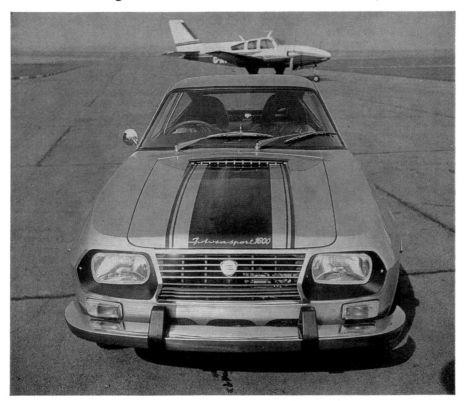

A 118 m.p.h. performer now available in Britain. Powered by the rally winning 1.6HF engine, standard specification includes many new and luxurious refinements aimed at the discriminating motorist. Price is £2592.23 including purchase tax. The Zagato is also available with a 1300 cc engine at £2145.15 including purchase tax.

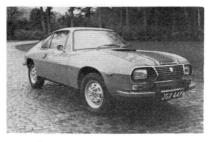

See the new Zagato in our showrooms now

What a perfect day
for trying out the Mercedes-Benz 280SE!

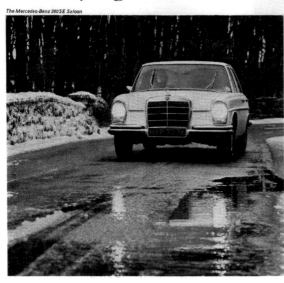

The Mercedes-Benz 280 SE Saloon

Bad weather is the acid test for any car. How it starts. How it handles. How safe it is.

That's why we invite you to choose the bleakest day this month to call us and arrange a drive in the Mercedes 280SE.

It starts first time, *every* time—even at a temperature of 20° below. Windscreens quickly clear for instant visibility.

Feel the superior holding power, the calm cornering, no matter how winter-ravaged the road. There are powerful four-wheel disc brakes for safe sure stopping even under the most extreme conditions.

Rain, Wind or Shine, come in anyway. It's the prime time for trying a Mercedes. The prime time for talking car. Talking price and taking ownership.

Mercedes-Benz: the end of compromise

ROBINSON'S AUTOSTAR GARAGE LTD.,
Riverside Road, Norwich Tel: Norwich 27134

Over on Riverside Road, you could have tried out the new Mercedes at Robinson's. Sure there's an element of safety features in some of this advertising, but really it's all about power and performance.

We'd like to demonstrate the 280E.
A twin-cam fuel injection Mercedes-Benz
with <u>added muscle!</u>

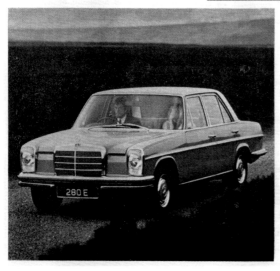

Added muscle
Introducing the powerful new 2.8 litre 185DIN h.p. twin overhead camshaft engine with electronic fuel injection and transistorised ignition.

Your introduction to the 280E will be quite a discovery, for this is a high performance car in every way. It's a car with power at a premium. Swift acceleration that puts just 9.8 seconds between standstill and 60 m.p.h., that continues right up the scale until top speed smoothly whispers in at around 125 m.p.h. (where the law allows) — that's power! But you'll find it's power perfectly balanced with control. Larger brakes, big radial tyres, controls and instruments positioned for safety and comfort combine to give supremely sure handling whatever your speed, whatever the road conditions.

Just telephone and we'll gladly arrange a test drive for you in the new 280E or its equally powerful stablemate the new 280CE Coupé. Recommended price for the Mercedes-Benz 280E is £3775.

ROBINSON'S AUTOSTAR GARAGE LTD.,
Riverside Road, Norwich Tel: Norwich 27134

With all credit to the advertisers, this message sends a clear signal that you could only enjoy the outstanding performance of the car within the law. The 70 mph speed limit would not become fully enforced until 1978. Prior to that, the 1970s had been something of a legal minefield for the motorist. In Norwich, as everywhere else in the UK, drivers had become used to petrol shortages as the various international crises took their stranglehold. Many were the queues at petrol stations across the city as drivers tried to fill up before stocks ran out. In an attempt to reduce fuel consumption, the government had introduced a 50 mph limit in December 1973. The temporary speed limits were extended in 1976 and increased to 60 mph in 1977. By June that year you were allowed to drive at 70 mph on motorways only.

The other factor for Norwich motorists to consider was Traffic Wardens. They'd been present in the city since the late 1960s. In 1973 they were equipped with motorbikes!

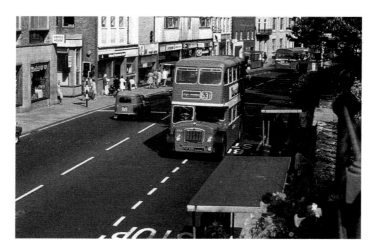

Castle Meadow, 1975. (Photograph courtesy of Stuart Ray)
    Often seen as another 'bus station', Castle Meadow was as busy as ever in the 70s.

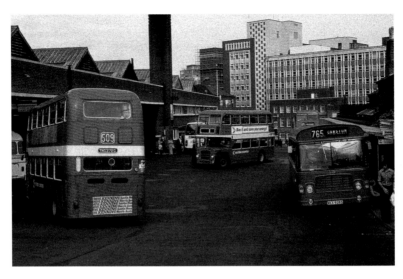

Meanwhile, in 1979 the 'real' bus station in Surrey Street was as busy as ever! (Photograph by Crewcastrian)

For those using public transport, the 1970s was still an era when Norwich buses were in their bright red livery. Castle Meadow was a vital shopping and changeover point for hundreds of bus passengers and routes; and of course it was still open to other traffic. Even the predicted increase in road use, and the measures put in place during the 1960s, hadn't enforced limited use of this busy thoroughfare by the mid-1970s.

This was still the age of drivers and conductors as two-man-crews on most buses. Incredibly by modern standards it was also still a time when passengers were allowed to smoke in the upstairs 'saloon' of the double deckers!

Opposite: The Maids Head Hotel. (Courtesy of Elliott Brown, under Creative Commons 2.0)

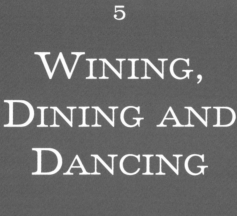

5

WINING, DINING AND DANCING

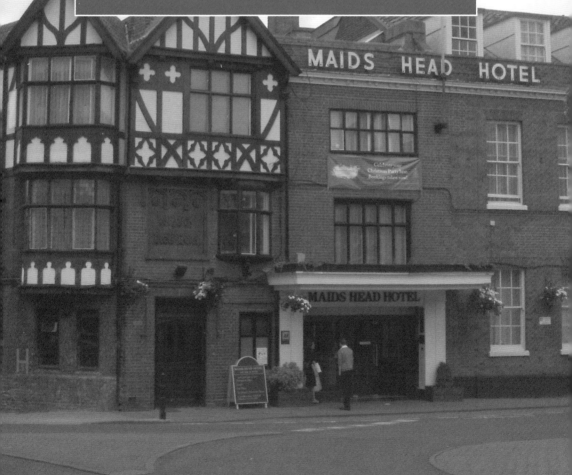

Certainly one of the primary recreational uses of the car in the 1970s was to go out for a drink and a meal. Today the very words 'drink' and 'drive' sit together very uneasily, and it's not to say that in general the 1970s motorist behaved irresponsibly. But, the idea of driving out to a pub, or restaurant, just outside the city for an evening meal was very much part of 70s culture.

And it was a culture that was changing. Famed for having a pub for every day of the year (the 365 pubs set against the equally famous 52 churches, one for every week of the year), Norwich embraced the social changes of the 1970s with open arms.

Whilst many city centre pubs retained their traditional approach of serving a range of beers, wines and spirits with limited if at all, food, some began to see the increased business available through 'pub grub'.

Chief among their new competitors though was the steakhouse. And none was more popular than the Berni. From Tombland to Thorpe, the red logo of the Berni steakhouses now offered a new experience. A good steak dinner was not new to Norwich diners. Gundry White's had long provided just that. But this was the age of the prawn cocktail, the steak and chips washed down with rosé wine, and of course Black Forest Gateau to finish. And the Berni offered it all. For many it would be their first experience of 'dining out' as adults.

On Tombland, Norwich's 'London Steak House' was the total Berni experience. Often booked to capacity, it served the classic meals, offering as a pre-dinner drink the dangerously large 'Schooner' of sherry.

Just outside the city centre, the fashionable 1970s fare could be had at the Boat and Bottle. To its credit, it had adopted the fashionable name just before the 70s began. Originally it had traded as Thorpe Gardens, but changed its name in 1969. The Boat and Bottle said it all. A trendy name and 1970s food. This was open-plan dining on several levels with a river view. This was the 70s.

Hotels had, of course, provided fine dining for years. In the case of the Maid's Head, since 1272. One of England's oldest inns, it celebrated

700 years of trading in 1972 and this advertisement ran at the time to announce the occasion. Just across the road from the Berni on Tombland, this proud hotel set out its stall, rightly claiming its heritage and its place in Norwich entertaining.

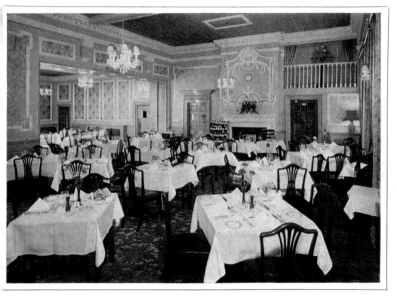

A relative newcomer to the Norwich hotel and dining scene was the Hotel Nelson. Unashamedly modern, it positively welcomed the driver into its Prince of Wales Road covered car park.

The Nelson had rapidly established itself as one of *the* places, especially for business people to lunch and dine.

It too, in stark modern contrast of approach to the Maid's Head, set out its pitch to customers, and it did it with a certain style.

'How many first class restaurants are there in East Anglia?' it asked, before saying that it wasn't for them to say but 'we do know that we top the list for sheer excellence of cuisine and elegance of décor'.

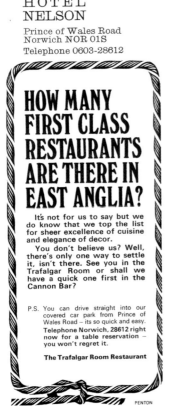

HOTEL
NELSON

Prince of Wales Road
Norwich NOR 01S
Telephone 0603-28612

HOW MANY FIRST CLASS RESTAURANTS ARE THERE IN EAST ANGLIA?

It's not for us to say but we do know that we top the list for sheer excellence of cuisine and elegance of decor.

You don't believe us? Well, there's only one way to settle it, isn't there. See you in the Trafalgar Room or shall we have a quick one first in the Cannon Bar?

P.S. You can drive straight into our covered car park from Prince of Wales Road – its so quick and easy. Telephone Norwich, 28612 right now for a table reservation – you won't regret it.

The Trafalgar Room Restaurant

PENTON

The Hotel Nelson sending out its message in 70s style.

Despite being aimed directly at the upmarket and business market, the Hotel Nelson was quick off the mark with a fast emerging 1970s idea. Pubs and restaurants were not child friendly in the 1970s, but the family Sunday lunch was catching on as part of the ever growing move towards eating out. There's no sign of the carvery that would soon typify such lunches; in fact this advertisement refers to the rather traditional *table d'hôte*, but the reference to family and reduced prices for children plainly sets this offer some distance from the licensed premises who as yet had not embraced, and indeed were not allowed to provide, family meals.

Between the Maid's Head on Tombland and the Hotel Nelson at the bottom of Prince of Wales Road, there was still the Castle Hotel. Long established, and in 1972 still offering 'Luncheon, Dinner and Private Parties of up to 100 ...', The Castle Hotel would succumb to demolition in 1990.

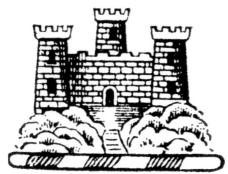

As the winds of cultural change blew through Norwich in the 1970s, that famous tally of 365 pubs was diminishing. During 1973 and 1974 alone, several famous establishments would hang up the towel for the last time. The Orford Arms, legendary for its live music, closed. Jimi Hendrix, the young Rod Stewart while with Long John Baldry's band and local hero Geno Washington had all played there. A favourite haunt of the 1960s mods it simply wasn't keeping pace with the 70s.

The Boar's Head in St Stephen's closed at roughly the same time, ending an era.

But before that, in 1971, a real Norwich institution came to an end. Backs was the name of a prominent family of vintners. Their trading went way back into the nineteenth century and had centred on premises on Gentleman's Walk, where they had both cellars and bottling facilities. On the ground floor was 'the bar'. Although it retained the name Backs, the firm had been owned by Hennekey's since the early 1950s. As a drinking place, it was unique. Huge barrels behind a massive bar and dark furniture showed it had made no concessions to the twentieth century, let alone the 1970s. During the 1920s, one pundit had said that going into Backs was like being transported back to the world of Good Queen Bess and Falstaff. There's no evidence to suggest that it changed in the ensuing fifty years.

However, the world, and Norwich, was changing. The once varied mix of customers started to fade away, and the main clientele had, by the late 60s, become mainly students from the University of East Anglia. Put bluntly, students did not have much money to spend and Backs began to experience a serious fall in profits. In a surprising move, suggestive of cutting off its nose to spite its face, they banned students. Profits of course fell further, but in an unexpected twist the students staged a protest at being banned. Even a 'sit in' failed to bridge the gap between the warring factions. It was going nowhere and to the horror of everyone, including those who'd probably not been in for years, Backs closed in 1971.

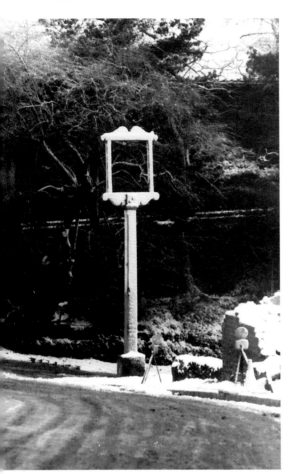
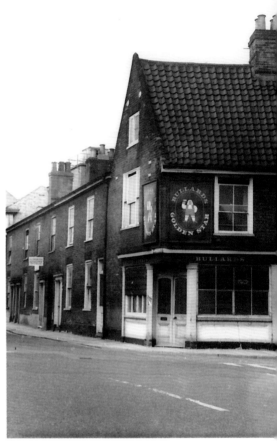

Above left: Gas Hill. An empty signboard says another pub closed. (Photograph courtesy of Paul Harley)

Above right: The Golden Star. Still showing its Bullard's branding. (Photograph courtesy of Paul Harley)

There was no doubt that the die had been cast. Food was what the new consumer wanted. Of course some of the traditional, old fashioned even, pubs survived, but many either converted to the new tastes or shut.

In an interesting link to the previous chapter, it was Pointer Motor Company who provided an unusual dining experience, and one possibly unique to Norwich. The Horseless Carriage was a restaurant inside a motor showroom. With booths styled as vintage cars, and food very much in the style of the times, it was hugely popular and talked of fondly to this day.

The Horseless Carriage – a truly unusual dining experience!

Cafés were suffering in much the same way as many pubs. Changing tastes and different expectations were posing a real threat to the Copper Kettles and Clover Leaf Cafés that had been such an essential part of city life for decades. Now there were new places like the Wimpy Bar, and the Golden Egg. These national chains provided a shiny, brightly lit, pastel-coloured plastic alternative to the traditional cafés, and they appealed to a younger market too. Even that 1960s favourite, Purdy's, on the ground floor of the tower in Westlegate suddenly seemed out of date.

Norwich was well catered for by the new brands with Wimpy Bars in St Giles, St Stephen's and Prince of Wales Road. The Golden Egg, complete with its egg-shaped menus, opened up in St Stephen's.

Just as their 1950s and 1960s predecessors had done in the cafes of a previous era, a new generation of Norwich teenager would make a cup of Wimpy coffee last a long time. These were meeting places for

RIO-MAR

Tel. 22533

Licensed Restaurant
and Coffee House

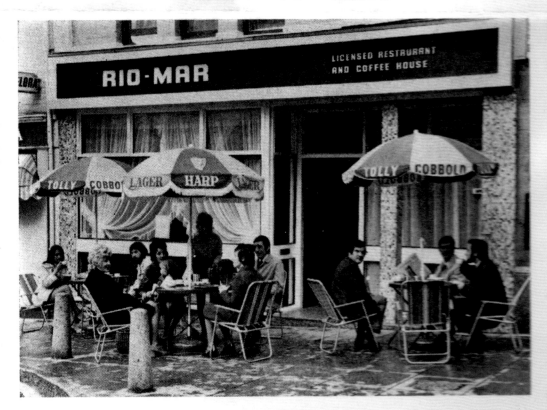

COFFEE HOUSE 9 a.m. to 6 p.m. Monday to Saturday
RESTAURANT 12 noon to 3 p.m. Monday to Saturday

Open Evenings 7 p.m. to 12 p.m.

55 LONDON STREET   -   -   NORWICH

Not all the independent cafés in Norwich were behind the times. The very modern, 1970s Rio Mar in London Street.

those too young for the pub, and not yet particularly interested in a three-course steakhouse dinner. The food was not expensive, and it introduced a generation to the burger.

Burgers weren't entirely new. The Americans had brought them over here during the war, and they were available in all sorts of places, including 'King Beefy', a mobile burger van that had satisfied the hunger of many a late night city drinker or club goer.

But something different was about to happen.

Mike Howell had been a salesman for Lotus. He had no experience in catering, or running any kind of restaurant. But he did have vision. Convinced that there was a gap in the market for a different kind of eating place, he started to do his research. He knew what he wanted as a customer, but he could seldom find it. It had to be in step with what he saw as the shift away from long, three or four-course meals. It had to be fun. It was probably going to serve hamburgers, but Mike knew that there was a vast difference between what he'd seen as a real American hamburger and the fare served by the chains. Or most other people.

It was all pointing towards an American style restaurant. At the age of twenty-two, in July 1972, Mike Howell opened Captain America's Hamburger Heaven in Exchange Street and started a legend.

From the outset Captain A's, as it was soon known, was different. Whilst the management always denied that it was policy, there could be no doubting that all the waitresses (there were no waiters) were very attractive, usually blonde and always dressed in the tightest jeans and shirts.

They served real American hamburgers like Norwich had never seen and, as the launch advertising stated, 'the heavenliest char-broiled American food you'll ever taste'.

American beers, iced water with your meal, good music playing constantly and a décor like no other meant eating out in the city had gone up a gear, and it was a unique Norwich business that had done it.

The footballers and local celebrities came in. People queued down the stairs and around the block to get in.

When Mike Howell had the idea of opening a bar upstairs, it was because he figured he could sell drinks to diners waiting for a table, and manage the size of the queue at the same time. He gave it a prohibition speakeasy theme and called it Skid Row. Norwich was about to discover cocktails!

The empire grew, tapping in to more and more of the 1970s fashion and tastes. On top of American food and cocktails there came Spangles, the city's first unisex hair salon.

Then it was Panache – a boutique that was totally on trend and in demand.

It's a sad fact that Mike Howell would not see the next development. Bistro Beano was planned for a location on Prince of Wales Road. On his way to sign the lease, Mike was killed in a car crash. He was twenty-five.

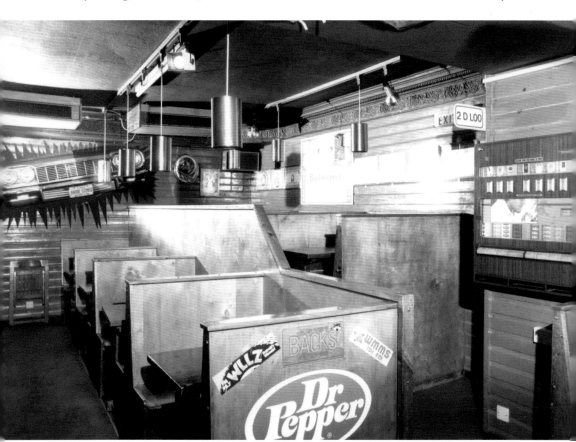

Inside Captain America's, 1972. Imported drinks, American-style booths and a car's front end – on the wall! It was all irresistible to Norwich in the 1970s. The cigarette machine leaps out of this picture when viewed over forty years later.

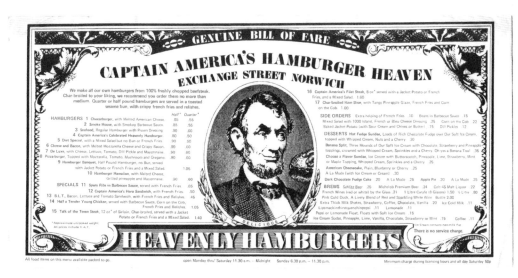

One of the now-famous early menus.

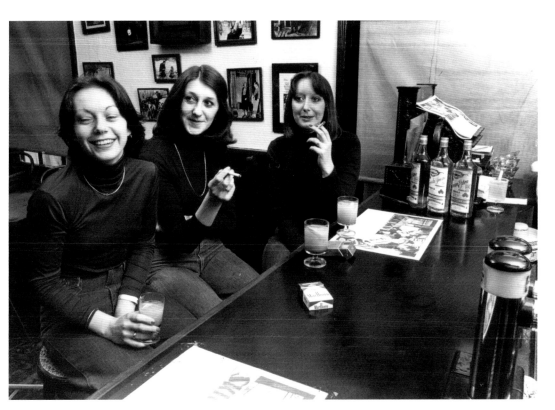

Skid Row. The bar upstairs at Captain America's, early 1970s.

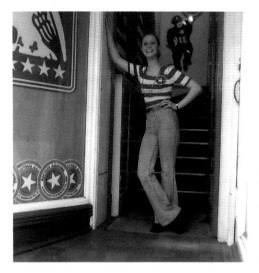

Lorraine Howes in the doorway of Captain America's at its July 1972 launch. She'd worked at Bonds and was nervous about joining this new, untried, restaurant business. She would stay for the next forty-three years.

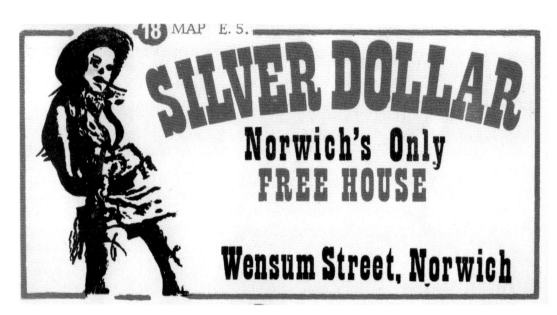

The Silver Dollar, which, amazingly, was Norwich's only free house in 1972. Such was the power of the breweries at that time, in an era when the choice of beers available was very narrow compared to the twenty-first century. 'A pint of bitter' or increasingly 'a pint of lager' was about all that was needed to be said when ordering!

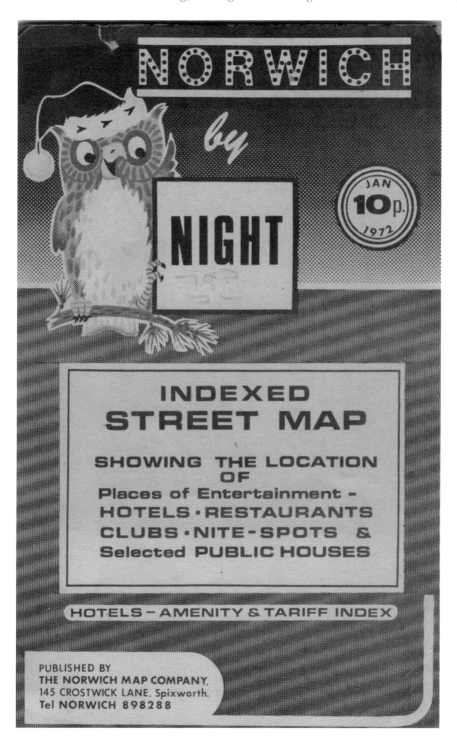

Norwich by Night, 1972.

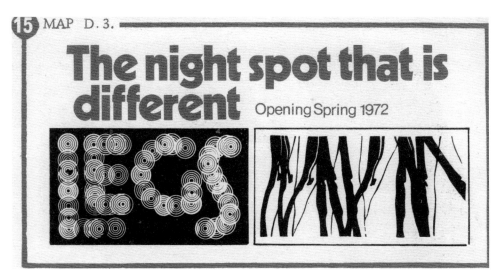

Legs.

By the early 1970s, Norwich had developed, in keeping with the national trends, a really quite diverse range of places for 'wining and dining' as well as enjoying the night life.

It could never have been totally comprehensive, but the 1972 'Norwich by Night' map and guide was a brave attempt to showcase the city's hot spots. A glimpse at some of the advertisements featured inside shows it is a revealing insight into Norwich in the early 1970s.

About as 70s trendy as you could get, despite being located in what could be seen as the less than fashionable Anglia Square, Legs soon became popular with footballers and celebrities and featured a private bar area – just for them. The club has worked itself into local folklore, and is still talked about today because of its advertising. There were problems with a club called Legs when you had to list opening and closing times!

'The Samson' was a long standing dance hall, or ballroom, and had been a favourite for generations of Norwich dancers. By the 1970s it was, not for the first time, re-inventing itself to cater for a changing public taste. 'Strict Tempo' still had a place, but was now relegated to Wednesday nights only. Monday offered a 'Discotheque'. These club sessions where a DJ played records instead of there being a live band

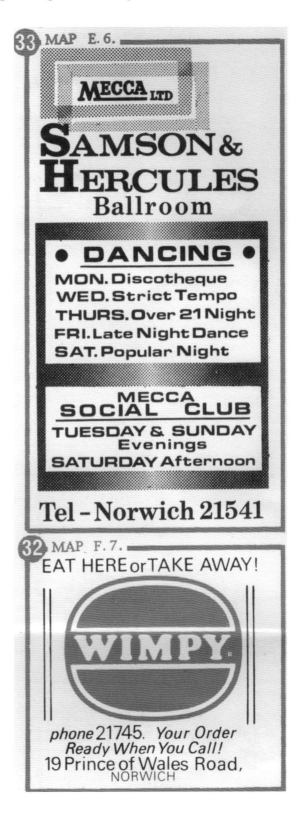

The Samson. And the Wimpy.

had taken hold in the 1960s, picking up on an idea first seen in the cellar clubs of late 1950s Paris. There was to be a huge leap from the musically impassioned but low-tech discotheques of the late 60s and early 70s to the laser and light effects of later years. Also, the fully spelled out, discotheque would evolve considerably, largely via New York, before its derivative, but massively popular descendant emerged as Disco!

From the 1940s onwards, for each decade, there's a generation of Norwich people who have their own particular memories of the Samson. The 1970s is no exception.

Immediately below to the Samson's ad is the one for the Wimpy. The Prince of Wales Road branch was just one of three or so in Norwich, and by the 70s would still have had to compete with the Grillette, which was next door to the ABC Cinema. Opening hours were not geared up for late-night suppers, but a new service had already been developed. You could telephone your order. (From a 'phone box of course!). Yes – 'Your Order Ready When You Call!' Very modern!

The Wimpy's other competitor, and unlike the Grillette, not just in Norwich, was the Golden Egg. They'd stretched opening times to midnight on Saturdays and Sundays. As an interesting footnote to life in 1970s Norwich, this establishment, based in St Stephen's, could point out that there was street parking available after 6.30pm!

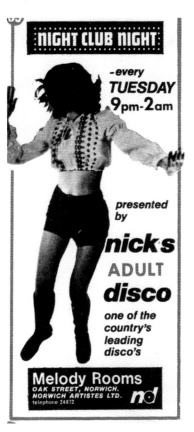

The Melody Rooms was the Oak Street Club that had thrived during the 1960s despite being known simply as the Industries Club, the Industrial Club, or by its die-hard audience as simply 'the Discotheque'. It had regularly featured nationally famous bands, but by 1972 was, like so many venues, offering a different kind of night out.

Already shortened to Disco, but not yet the world of Donna Summer and Abba, 'Nick's Adult disco' was a regular weekly event. The adult label had no suggestive element to it. This was simply saying 'it's not for young teenagers'. It was all part of the 70s. We're grown up. We go out to dinner. We go to clubs. We probably drink Blue Nun.

Club America in Lobster Lane was another of the clubs that strived to deliver a sophisticated nightclub atmosphere to the 1970s audience. Not the biggest place in the city, but hugely popular, the club developed an impressive reputation.

6
STEPPING OUT IN 70S STYLE

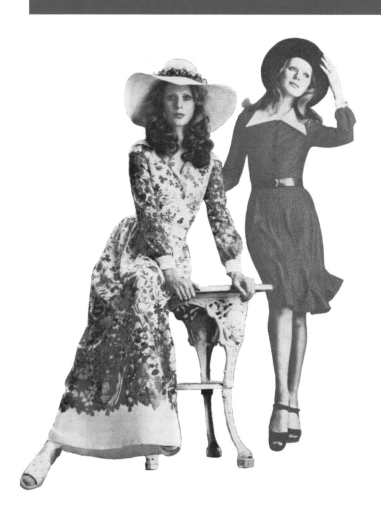

The ten years of the 1970s saw a huge shift in fashions and taste. On the streets of Norwich, it was evident in the changing face of retail. Just as with furnishings and home interiors, the 1970s brought new shops, and some serious changes to existing ones.

The 1960s had ended with the two big fashion cults of the decade going their own ways. The rockers would still hang around at the 3Cs and their favourite cafés, and their overall look had not changed much. The mods had moved on from Purdy's in Westlegate, the Gala and the Industrial Club in Oak Street. They still had Harry Fenton in St Stephen's, and Jackson the Tailor on Gentleman's Walk to supply them with their suits, and several local shops including Anderson's for their Levis. But those of them who still had the obsession for clothes that had defined them were looking for something new. Some, only a few, looked towards a more floral style.

The late 60s had seen the flowering of the hippie and their needs in Norwich were soon to be satisfied by Head in the Clouds. Opened in 1971, the shop embraced all that was love and groovy, as it does to this day. Many a mainstream retailer has floundered in the forty years and more since Head in the Clouds was seen by them as a short-lived novelty. Britain's oldest head shop still goes on.

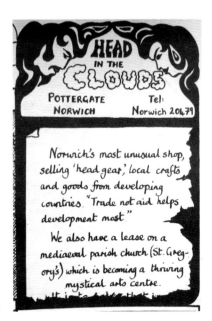

Head in the Clouds.

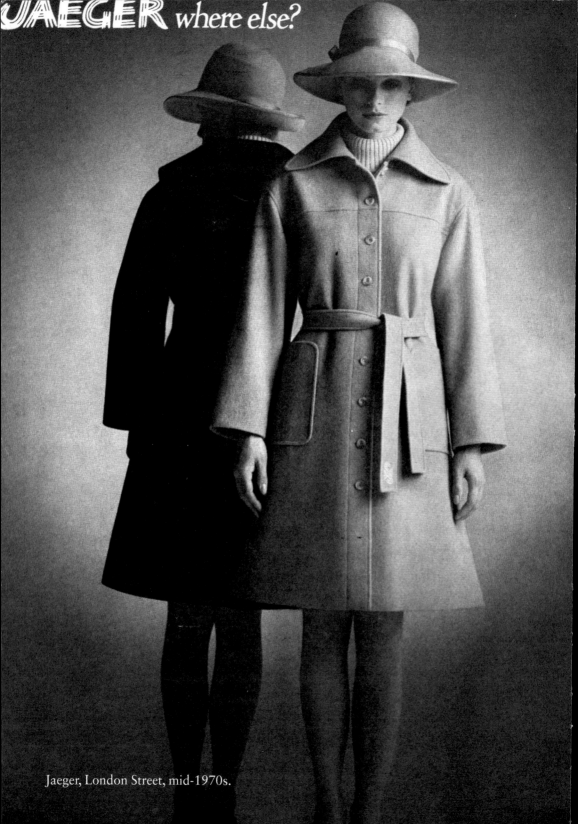

JAEGER *where else?*

Jaeger, London Street, mid-1970s.

In the mainstream Norwich was well appointed. By now Jaeger had opened their store in London Street and their relatively expensive but well-made clothes soon helped characterise the style of the 70s. Still under the original name, Bond's were embracing the 70s with style too. Redolent of Biba and pared down to a simple look, their mid-1970s advertising was exactly right for the times.

Bond's celebrated their centenary in 1979. Along with Jarrold's, one of the city's only two family-owned department stores, they had extended their floor space as part of a major refurbishment.

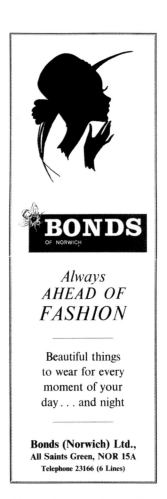

BONDS
OF NORWICH

Always
AHEAD OF
FASHION

Beautiful things
to wear for every
moment of your
day . . . and night

Bonds (Norwich) Ltd.,
All Saints Green, NOR 15A
Telephone 23166 (6 Lines)

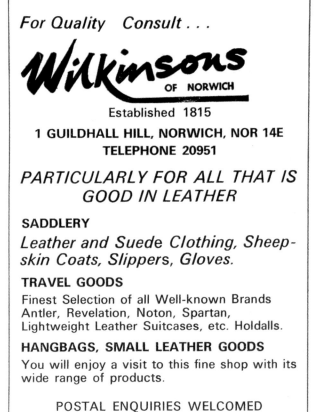

For Quality Consult . . .

Wilkinsons OF NORWICH

Established 1815

1 GUILDHALL HILL, NORWICH, NOR 14E
TELEPHONE 20951

PARTICULARLY FOR ALL THAT IS
GOOD IN LEATHER

SADDLERY
Leather and Suede Clothing, Sheep-
skin Coats, Slippers, Gloves.

TRAVEL GOODS
Finest Selection of all Well-known Brands
Antler, Revelation, Noton, Spartan,
Lightweight Leather Suitcases, etc. Holdalls.

HANGBAGS, SMALL LEATHER GOODS
You will enjoy a visit to this fine shop with its
wide range of products.

POSTAL ENQUIRIES WELCOMED
OPEN SIX DAYS A WEEK

Above right: Perhaps a little less stylish in their advertising approach, but Wilkinson's was a much loved Norwich business. Their Guildhall Hill shop was *the* place to go to for sheepskin coats.

Key among the long-established retailers who were moving with the times was Jarrold's. The store in Exchange Street had been extended in 1964 when they built on the site of the old Corn Hall.

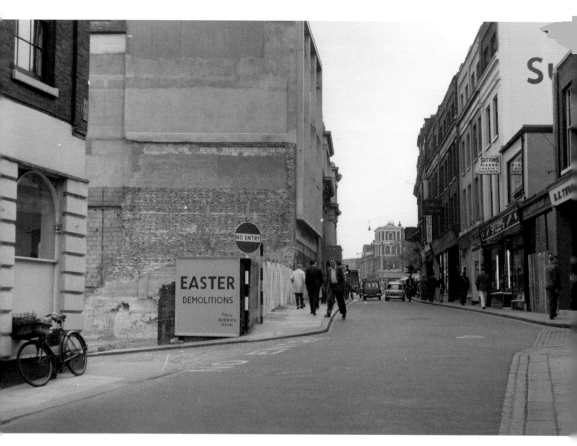

Photograph by the late Les Edwards and courtesy of Wayne Beauchamp.

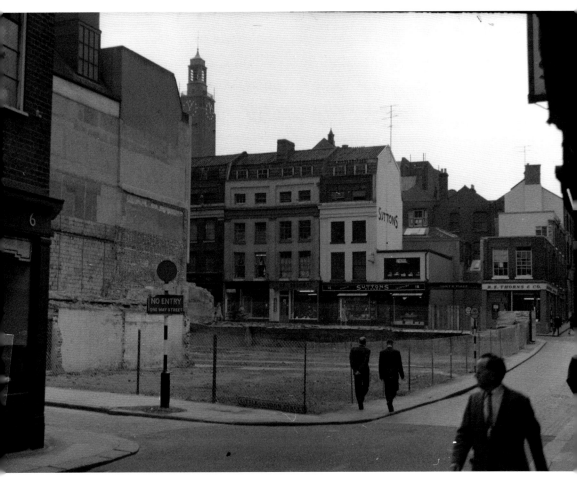

1964. Pre-dating the 1970s, but these pictures show not only the area created by the demolition of the Corn Hall, but also the space into which Jarrold's extended from Exchange Street to Bedford Street.

The newly increased floor space gave them the opportunity to widen their offering and, to the surprise of some, they created a fashion department. At the turn of the decade there had been the terror of the Garland's fire of 1970 which had come perilously close to Jarrold's, but no damage was sustained and by the early 70s the store was firmly in the fashion market.

This double-page spread from 1972 sets out the styles and trends for that spring. It's a confident statement from a leading retailer.

JARROLDS
Spring Fashions

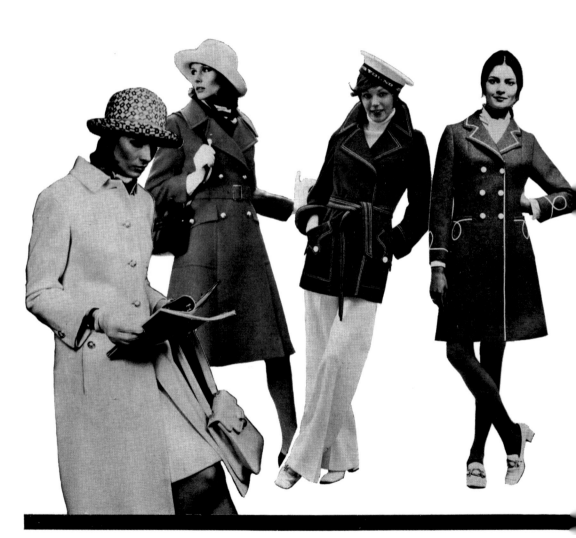

'Amanda' single - breasted spring coat in grey flannel or double jersey.
— By Aquascutum. £39.00

'Valencia' double breasted classic with patch pockets and belt in Worsted cloth.
— By Aquascutum. £42.00

'Naturally Navy' wrap-around jacket in grey, navy or black, all wool flannel with white stitching to high-light detail.
— By Alexon (Youngset) £17.50

'Nautical Flavour' dou[ble] breasted coat in grey b[lue] or navy pure wool flan[nel] outlined with white br[aid]
— By Alexon (Youngs[et]) £17.00

Spring evokes a longing for all things new, and this year you have the choice of being several kinds of person — with the "Navy Lark" catching on with its slick nautical trousers suits, complete with cheeky hats; two piece outfits with detachable sailor collars and smart fine wool coats with just a touch of braid to bring them into the 'sailor look' class.

Classics, timeless and chic as ever appear in bold colours. With these you must wear the new 'sea design' silk scarfs — just for a touch of fashion.

For evenings, parties and special occasions, dresses have never been more feminine and appealing — your menfolk will adore the soft florals and the long romantic styles in floaty voiles and chiffons.

Hats too are so beautiful — trimmed with luscious full blown silk roses and now once more — twirls of veiling.

So you really can take the choice this Spring and have a completely different look for day and evening.

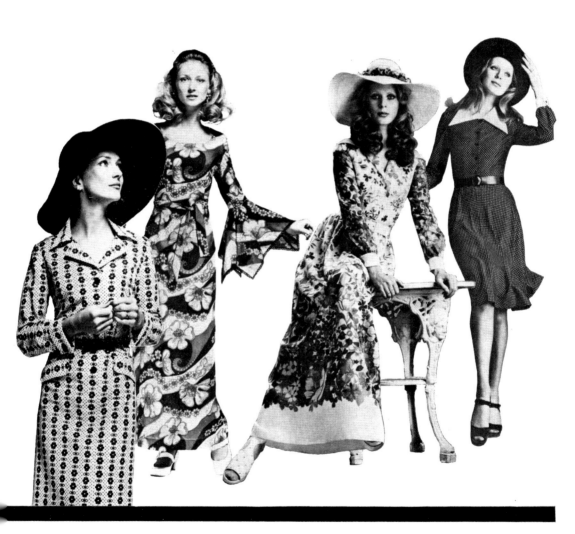

'Occasion' dress, classic shirtwaister in black, french navy or tomato on a natural ground, blended Polyester.
— By Horrockses. £9.50

'Glamour' slim fitting hostess dress in royal/olive/purple or black/mustard/cerise washable cotton with 'handkerchief' sleeves edged with lace.
— By Horrockses. £12.50

'Ascot' dress in shades of green and brown on white border printed cotton voile.
— By Polly Peck. £10.85

'Spring step out' dress in black, navy or yellow with white, cotton and viscose.
— By Polly Peck. £6.90

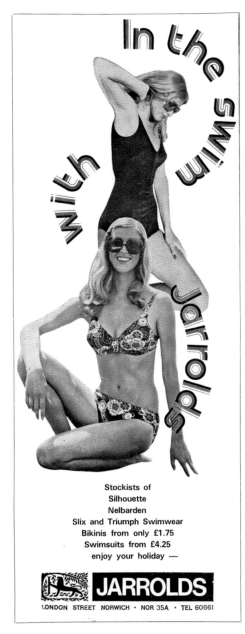

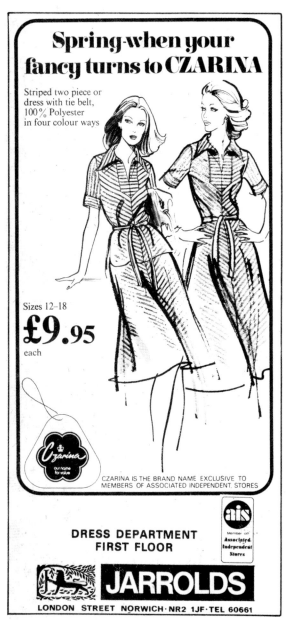

Above left: Still with female fashion in mind, and trading on those 1970s summers, Jarrolds were in the swim in July 1972.

Above right: Mid-1970s and Jarrolds have an entire department for dresses.

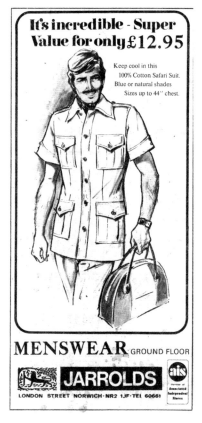

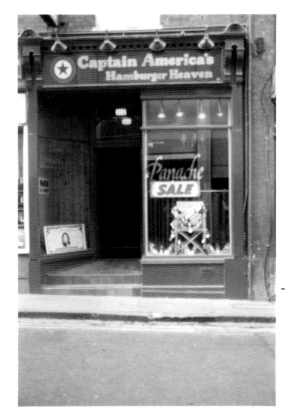

Above left: When it came to men's fashion, Jarrolds were there for the 1970s male. The safari suit is not remembered fondly but for a brief moment it was the very thing for spring and summer!

Above right: Panache – the Exchange Street boutique, and part of Captain America's.

Meanwhile, across the road on the other side of Exchange Street, Captain America's had moved into fashion, and opened their own boutique, Panache.

For ladies, the new places to shop just kept coming. Brands like Snob arrived in the city centre. Bond's, Curl's, Peter Robinson and, of course, Marks and Spencer all upped their game to compete with the new, usually smaller, competitors. By the mid-1970s a refurbished Garland's would heighten Norwich's shopping experience, and C&A had set up shop at the Haymarket to offer even more choice. (And often become

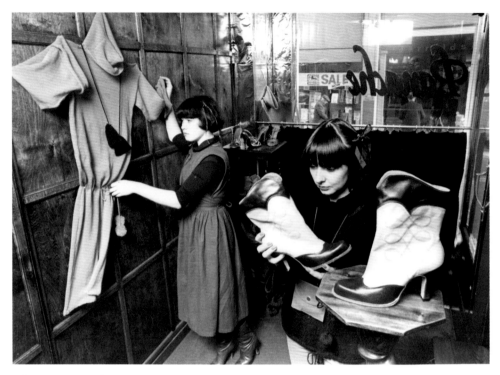

This picture, taken inside Panache and looking out towards Jarrold's, captures the boutique style and 70s look that characterised this highly popular new arrival on the fashion scene.

victim to the fountain outside it being treated with washing up liquid to create a spectacular bubbly display!)

As for the men, they were looking for more choice too. The 1960s hadn't exactly been short of style, but the 70s seemed to be getting off to a slow start. Names like Gaegen will strike a chord with those who remember the times. It typified the small, independent, shop selling stylish clothes against a backdrop of loud music and primitive changing rooms.

And just as the flares got wider and the lapels got sharper, another name stepped in to the ring: Jonathan Trumbull. Coming out of a long established firm of Norwich menswear retailers, and adopting a name that few questioned or inquired about, Jonathan Trumbull opened its doors in St Stephen's in March 1971.

Roger Kingsley and his brother, whose father ran the Chadd's clothes shop, had done something different. Just when the city was full of shops trying desperately to be modern, they created a place with a distinctively 'old world' interior.

It was a game changer. Now there was a place where the very latest clothes could be bought from a shop that felt special. It had everything. The suits, shoes, ties and shirts. The knitwear and the accessories. It was all there, and you were able to discuss it with people who talked about clothes with enthusiasm and knowledge.

Every action has a reaction. As the 1970s developed ever more stylish shops and clothes, and as the music shook off the long guitar solos and moved into a sequinned disco party, there was something else about to happen. And it didn't like sequins, or disco.

Punk was a scene that struggled to get a foothold in Norwich. The city had somehow found it easier to adopt the glamour and good times of the 70s than it had the spiky reaction to it.

A significant fact about punk in Norwich was that, unlike most other people who were part of the city's social life, it didn't centre on clubs. Nor restaurants for that matter.

The hub of punk activity was the pub. And it was pubs that were somehow just off the main city centre. Punks gravitated to the Woolpack in Muspole Street and the Golden Star.

Interestingly, there was one existing club the punks liked. It was The Jacquard. They liked it because it wasn't glamourous. Somehow the folk and blues tradition fitted with the new rebellion.

And it was in many ways a misunderstood rebellion. In fact the movement that was seen as snarling and dangerous was arguably really creative. Saturday mornings were often spent at jumble sales and second-hand shops to pick up old clothes that were then taken apart and remodelled with the obligatory zips and safety pins before setting off, to show off, on Saturday night.

Meeting in Pottergate, or Muspole Street, sinking a few beers and maybe calling in to People's in Westlegate, or Oats in Bedford Street, were the precursors to that essential activity of gate crashing a Saturday night party. More interested in beer than drugs, and obsessed with the music that was at the core of punk, they went the way of most cults. The purists, there at the start, began to resent the inevitable acceptance of the mainstream. When you could buy ready-made punk clothes from a chain store it was, in the eyes of the real devotees, over.

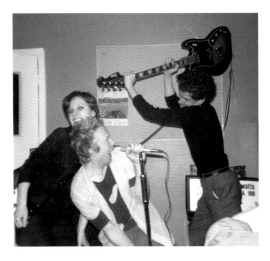

Left and below: Punks Norwich, late 1970s. (Photographs courtesy of Jonty Young)

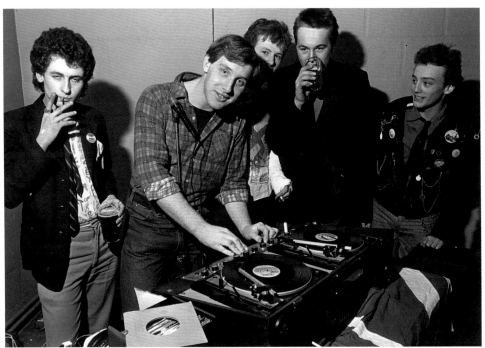

If, though, there is a moment when punk and the establishment went head to head it would have to be the Royal Jubilee in 1977. Norwich typified the melting pot that now defined the country. While well-dressed young people queued at the Samson and the Norwood Rooms to strut their stuff to mainstream music, and the Sex Pistols railed against the monarchy, the city engaged in the celebration of Her Majesty's twenty-five years on the throne.

June 1977 saw a citywide range of events. The Lord Mayor's Street Procession on 4 June attracted huge crowds. Fêtes and festivals were the order of the day.

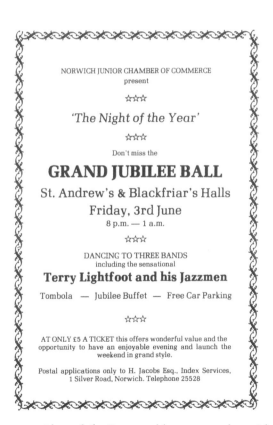

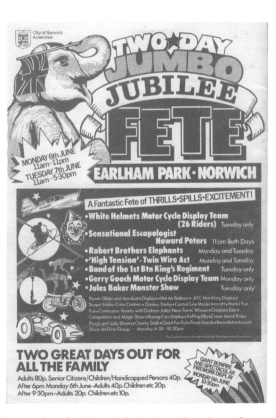

Above left: Presumably not popular with the punks, the Norwich Junior Chamber of Commerce kicked off the Jubilee celebrations with a Trad Jazz Ball.

Above right: The Jumbo Jubilee Fête in Earlham Park.

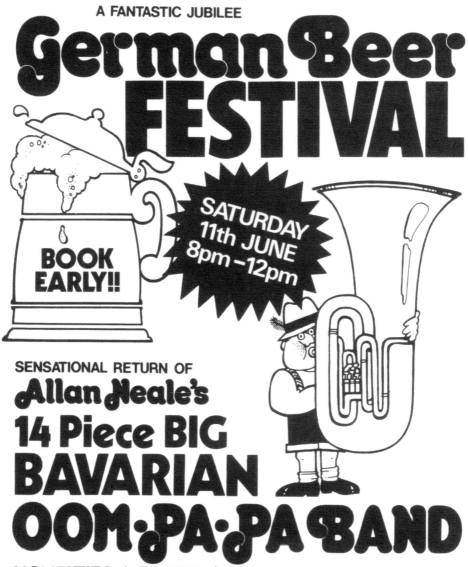

A FANTASTIC JUBILEE

German Beer FESTIVAL

BOOK EARLY!!

SATURDAY 11th JUNE 8pm-12pm

SENSATIONAL RETURN OF

Allan Neale's

14 Piece BIG BAVARIAN OOM·PA·PA BAND

NOVELTIES ☆ PRIZES ☆ RAFFLE, ETC.

St. Andrews Hall, Norwich

TICKETS £1·50 from Go Places Travel, Exchange Street (opposite Jarrolds);
Amenities Office, 15 Chapel Field East (closed Sat and 1–2 pm daily)
& St. Andrews Hall (closed Sat and 1–2pm daily)
Tourist Information Centre, Tombland.

FOR PARTY BOOKING
Tel: 22233 Ext. 563

GERMAN BEER • NOVELTIES • PARTY FUN

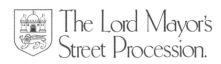

The Lord Mayor's Street Procession.

JUDGES:
Lord and Lady Mayoress - Councillor and Mrs Ralph Roe
The Rt Hon David Ennals, M.P.
Mr John Garrett, M.P.
The Right Reverend the Lord Bishop of Norwich
The Right Reverend Bishop K. Sansbury
Mr C.G. Taylor, Q.P.M. Chief Constable of Norfolk
Mr Martin Chase - President of Norwich Chamber of Commerce
Heather Stutter 'Scope' Eastern Evening News
Maureen Holden - British Showjumping Team Member

A collection will be held for the City of Norwich Jubilee Fund.

Contributions will be shared equally between Local and National
Youth Projects serving the Community.
Please give generously.
During the Procession over 100 FREE TICKETS for the Jumbo
Jubilee Fete will be given to Boys and Girls seen waving Union
Jacks.

DON'T FORGET to follow the Procession to the CATHEDRAL
and join in its special OPEN EVENING then come along to THE
CITY CENTRE where there will be entertainment and events
until Midnight. See Programme Diary for full details.

The Procession's Organisers would like to thank our Judges and
the many organisations and individuals who have either taken
part or have made the Parade possible. The invaluable co-operation
of the Police and other services is also acknowledged. To those
who may be inconvenienced please accept our apologies but we
are sure you will appreciate that celebrations of this nature do
not happen very often.

**PLEASE WAVE YOUR FLAGS. CHEER YOUR FLOATS AS
LOUDLY AS POSSIBLE. GIVE GENEROUSLY AND
ABOVE ALL
ENJOY YOURSELVES**

24

Route.

Saturday, June 4th 1977, 7.30 p.m.
Theme NORWICH in 1977
Prizes (kindly donated by Norwich Chamber of Commerce)
1st £25, 2nd £15, 3rd £10, Highly Commended

CLASS A — COMMERCIAL
CLASS B — CHARITABLE
VOLUNTARY ORGANISATIONS
PRIVATE ENTRIES

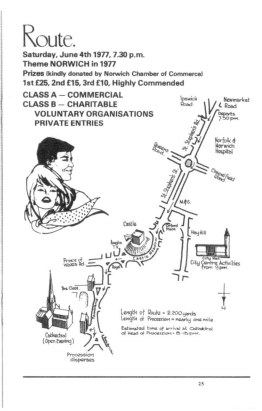

Length of Route = 2,200 yards
Length of Procession = nearly one mile.

Estimated time of arrival at Cathedral
of head of Procession - 8.15 p.m.

25

The official Lord Mayor's Street Procession – with instructions to enjoy yourselves!

In fact, the Lord Mayor's Procession had only recently made a return to the streets of Norwich, largely as the brainchild of Harry Boreham at the *Eastern Daily Press*, who wanted to create a continental style event, but drawing on the city's heritage, including Snap the dragon.

Opposite: In St Andrew's Hall, the Jubilee was celebrated with a German Beer Festival.

Next page: City Hall, Norwich. (Courtesy of Trojan_Llama, under Creative Commons 2.0)

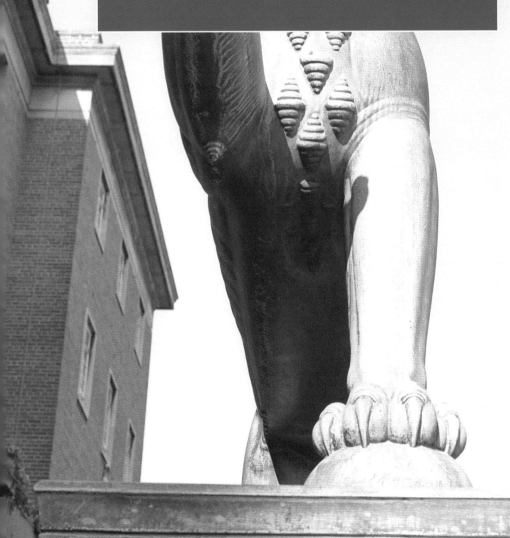

7

DRAWING TO
A CONCLUSION

The intention of this book has been to take an affectionate look over the shoulder at Norwich in the 1970s. It could only ever be a glimpse at those ten years, because so much happened during them.

For the ever loyal fans of Norwich City Football Club, there is an entire, and excellent, book by Edward Couzens-Lake, on the team's achievements and developments in those years. In his *Norwich City: The Seventies*, he chronicles their rise to national recognition. The heartbreak of losing the 1973 League Cup Final would not mar their overall progress in the decade.

For those who recall the seventies as a time of power cuts and three-day weeks, Norwich in those days may hold memories of hard times and bleak winters. Yes, there was industrial unrest, from the Post Office to Laurence Scott and Electromotors, but there were also long hot summers, new shops and an optimism that today fuels some of the fondest memories.

The University of East Anglia gained an international reputation and major bands played the city's venues.

At the very start of the decade, in 1970, Air Anglia arrived to begin a new era. As the decade closed it merged with rivals to form Air UK.

'And now – live from Norwich' became a national catchphrase as the *Sale of the Century* grew into one of the most successful and most watched game shows on national television. There were bargains to be had at BB Adams and Fine Fare arrived to shake up the supermarket scene.

Memories of 1976 are often centered on that particularly hot summer, and it's interesting to note that they've somehow cancelled out the weather of earlier that year. Norwich made national news in January 1976 when every road out of the city was blocked by the horrendous storm that uprooted over 600 trees.

And as the 70s drew to a close, another event propelled Norwich into the national awareness. On 6 December 1979, some 120 people, instantly labelled as 'squatters' moved into Argyle Street. They set up

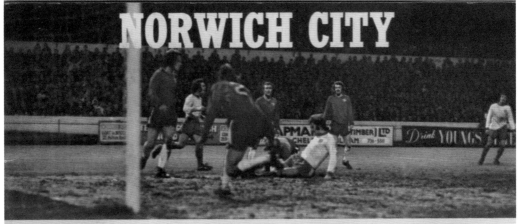

 THE FOOTBALL LEAGUE

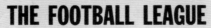

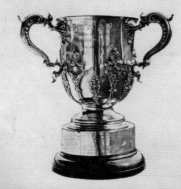

CUP

**SATURDAY
3rd MARCH
1973**

FINAL

**KICK
OFF
3.30 pm**

TOTTENHAM HOTSPUR

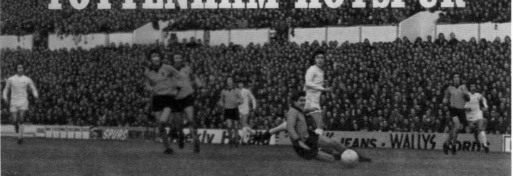

Official Programme Ten Pence   Incorporating Cup Final Issue of "League Football"

 WEMBLEY
EMPIRE STADIUM

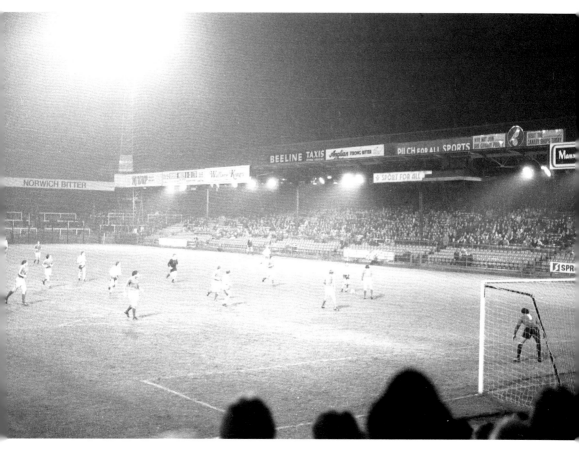

A glimpse of another memory. Norwich City play the rest of the world in a 1979 testimonial. (Photograph courtesy of Andrew Wenley)

Opposite: The League Cup Final, 1973. Not a victory, but it didn't mar the team's overall success throughout the decade.

home there and became known as the Argyle Street Alternative Republic. Their high profile eviction in 1985 was filmed and it would emerge later as the documentary *Street of Experience*.

Suddenly, there was to be a General Election – and the 70s were over. 1979 saw a General Election result that would change so much.

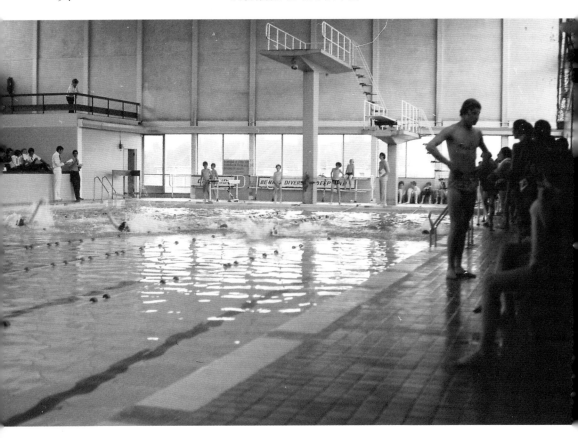

St Augustine's swimming pool, 1970s. (Photograph courtesy of Andrew Wenley)

Whilst you could cool off in the still open air pool at Lakenham, or paddle at Wensum Park, swimming was still centred on the pool at St Augustine's. In the 70s this was still seen as something of a 'new' building, having arrived in the 1960s. Local clubs used it, and it was hugely popular with city residents in an era when gym membership was not really on the agenda.

Many Norwich people will have learned to swim in the St Augustine's pool, many of them taken there by their school. It's odd to think that a place so fondly remembered by countless Norwich people was so short-lived.

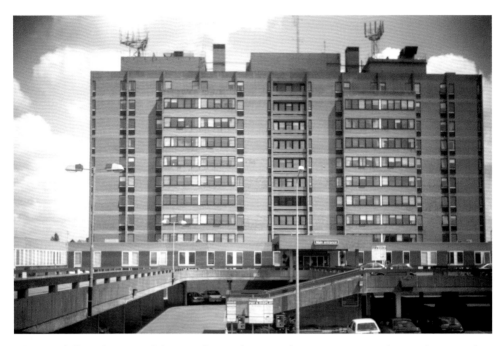

The Norfolk and Norwich hospital, seen here in what many Norwich people remember as the 'new buildings' was yet another piece of the 70s that has not survived.

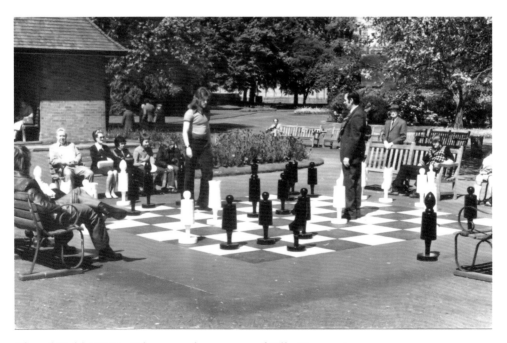

Chapel Field, 1970s. (Photograph courtesy of Olly Downes)
   For those looking for a more sedate and open-air form of relaxation during the hot 1970s summers there was the giant chess board in Chapel Field park.

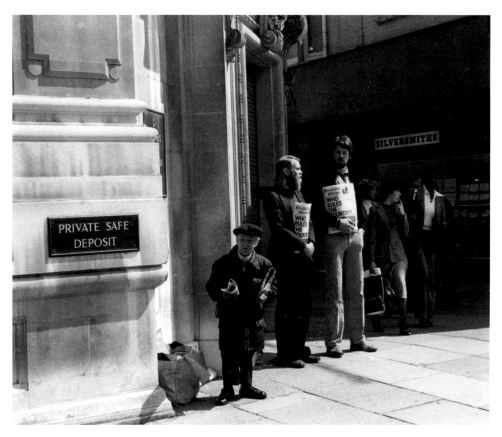

1979, election time, and the *Socialist Worker* is on offer on the city's streets, as well as the local press. (Photograph courtesy of Paul Harley)

The 1980s were just around the corner and the 70s would, perhaps more than most decades, slip quickly into history. The styles and tastes of those ten years would soon seem wildly out of step with the 80s.

It's odd to reflect that 1975 was only thirty years after the end of the Second World War. At time of writing, it's forty years ago. Those forty years have suddenly made what some called 'the decade that taste forgot' a time of nostalgia. If you weren't around then, I hope this book will have given you just a hint of what life was like in Norwich in the 1970s. If you were around – I hope it's stirred some memories.